HeSS

CAM

Published in the United States of America
by Rand McNally & Company, 1983.

© Grisewood & Dempsey Limited, 1983.

Printed and bound by Graficas Reunidas SA, Madrid, Spain.

Second printing, 1984

ISBN 0 528 82389-2

Library of Congress Catalog Card No. 83–61911.

Consultant: Ellen Nevins
Supervisor of Computer-based Education
AT & T Long Lines
Corporate Education and Training Organization
Piscataway, New Jersey

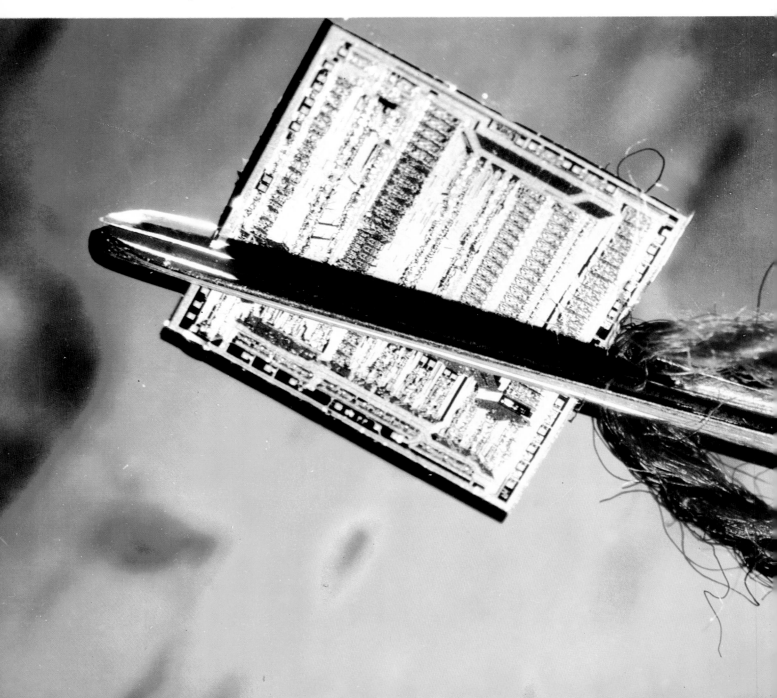

ENCYCLOPEDIA OF
Computers
and
Electronics

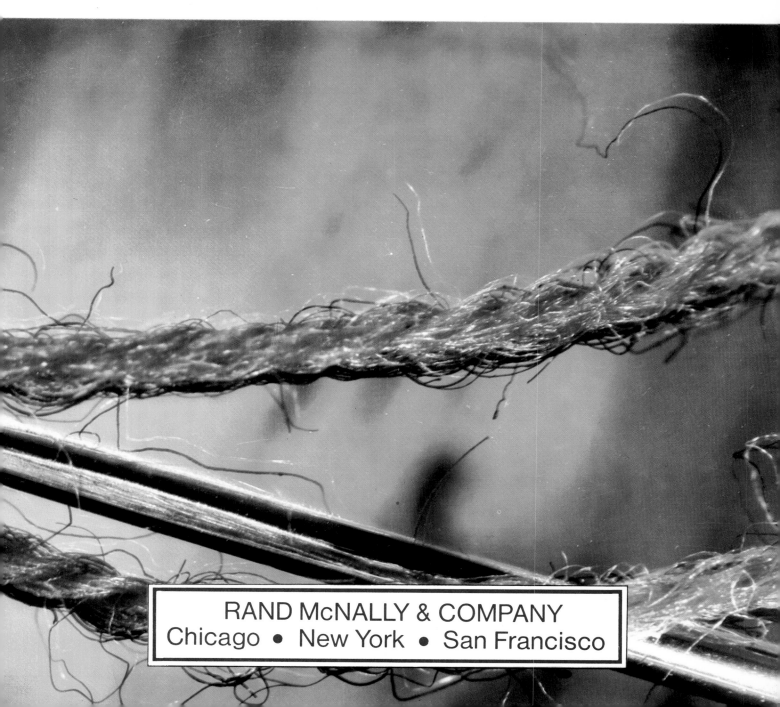

RAND McNALLY & COMPANY
Chicago • New York • San Francisco

Contents

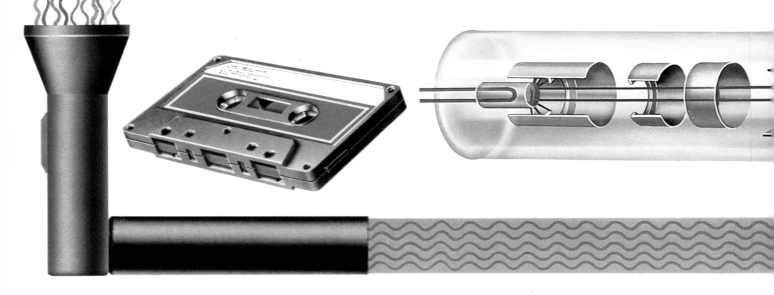

Electronic This and That

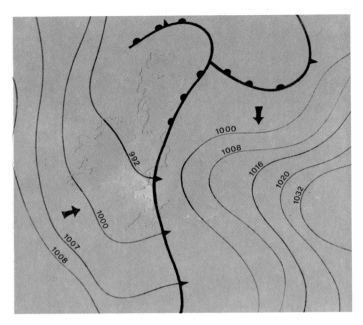

Computers are being used more and more in a wide variety of tasks. Weather maps (above) are worked out by big computers that are fed with information from all over the world. Pilots training in simulators see views of runways that are the creation of computers (below). Many of their instruments are computer-controlled too.

The computer and electronics have now become a part of all our lives. Every day we hear people talking about "silicon chips," "microelectronics," "computer programs" and electronic this and that. We have tiny portable television sets, digital watches, videos, home computers, calculators and colorful computer games. Even our washing machines and office typing equipment have small computers inside them to make work easier.

All these things have become possible because the parts inside them have become smaller and smaller and use less and less electricity. Without these tiny devices, we would not have been able to land on the Moon or send probes hurtling through space to look at and send back information from the distant planets.

In this book we will take a look at computers to find out what they can do and how they do it. We will also discover how many other electronic devices work and the wonderful things they can do for us.

It is with "electronics" that we must begin.

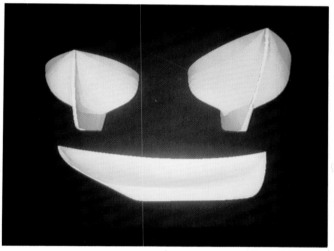

The heart of the computer is the silicon chip. The picture above shows a slice of silicon containing hundreds of these tiny marvels. Cartoon films can be computer-drawn (above right), while the computer can also design complicated shapes and show us the shape from different angles (right). Computers are a vital part of industrial design (below).

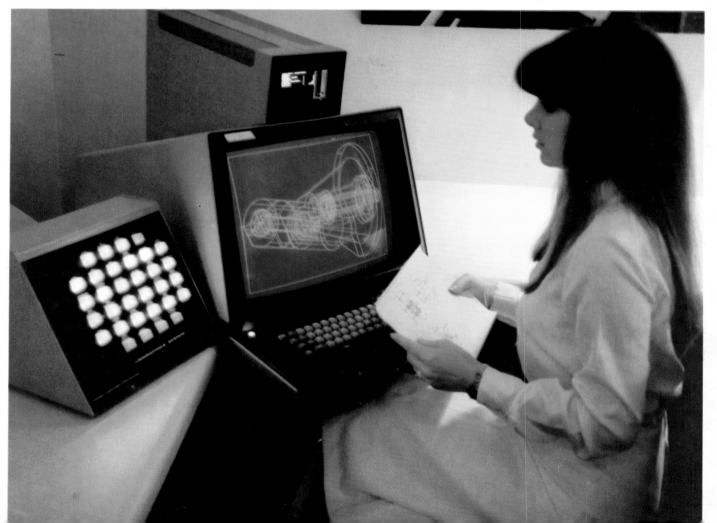

Electrons Everywhere

The center of an atom is made up of protons and neutrons. Around these whizz electrons. Each element has a different number of protons, neutrons and electrons. The picture on the right represents a carbon atom. It has 6 of each.

Electrons

Protons

Neutrons

The dictionary tells us that electronics is the branch of science that deals with the accurate control of electric currents. Radios, television sets, computers, tape recorders, radars, X-ray machines and pocket calculators are all electronic machines. Imagine the world without these devices and you will see how important electronics is to all of us.

What is an Electric Current?

Everything is made of tiny atoms. The Sun and the Earth and everything that lives is made up of atoms. But atoms are much too small to be seen. They are so small that about 250,000 million of them could be placed on the period that ends this sentence.

At the center of each atom is something that is called the *nucleus*. Around the nucleus spin other even tinier parts called *electrons*. The electrons circle the nucleus millions of times in a millionth of a second. They spin in different orbits around the center and they carry a tiny charge of negative electricity. Electricity can be *negative*, shown in writing by the minus sign —, or it can be *positive*, shown by the plus sign +.

The atoms of some substances have what are called *free electrons* – electrons that can jump from

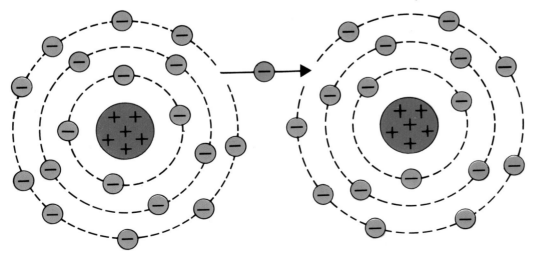

Electricity flows along a wire when electrons jump from one atom to the next. Electrons are tiny units of negative electricity. The protons in the center of the atoms are positive.

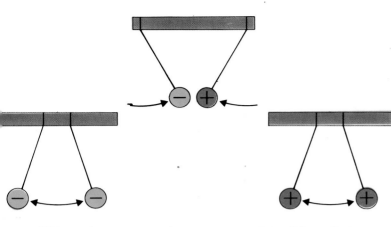

Things that are negative are attracted to things that are positive. Two negative things push each other apart. So do two positive things.

one atom to the next quite easily. When electrons flow in this way, there is an *electric current*. An electric current is a flow of electrons from one place to another. Every metal has free electrons, but some metals have more than others. Metals carry electricity; they are *conductors*.

When an electric current flows along a wire, especially a wire made from a metal that does not let the current pass too easily, the free electrons bump against the atoms in the wire and make it hot. As the wire gets hotter, the electrons move faster and faster, and more electrons are knocked from their atoms. Some of the electrons move so fast that they escape from the wire altogether. Then they hang around the wire like a cloud of bees.

Negative and Positive Electricity

There is one important rule that applies to everything electrical. Things with a negative electric charge are pulled towards things with a positive electric charge. Two things with a positive charge push each other apart. So do two things with a negative charge.

Streams of Electrons

When electrons escape from a hot piece of metal, they are pulled towards anything that is positively charged. (Electrons are negative; positive and negative charges attract each other.) The electrons flow from the hot metal to the positively charged object in a steady stream.

Electronics is all about controlling streams of electrons.

Vacuum Tubes

In 1904, a British engineer called Ambrose Fleming made the first successful electron tube. A vacuum tube is a glass or metal tube that has all the air pumped out of it, and it may contain small amounts of other gases. Sealed in the tube are a *cathode* that is heated by an electric current and a plate or *anode* that is made positive so that it attracts electrons from the cathode. This kind of tube is called a *diode* because it has two parts inside it – di means two.

In the diode, electrons flow from the cathode to the anode. But they only flow when the anode is made positive. Electrons do not flow if the anode has a negative charge.

The electricity that comes from the electrical sockets in our walls is *alternating current* or AC – it flows one way then the other, changing from negative to positive 60 times every second. But many machines such as television sets and radios can only work on *direct current* – DC – current that always flows in the same direction.

We use diodes to change AC into DC. This is why they are sometimes called valves – they only allow the current to flow through them one way. The valve in a car or bicycle tire allows air to be pumped in but does not let it out. We have valves in our hearts that only allow our blood to flow in one direction.

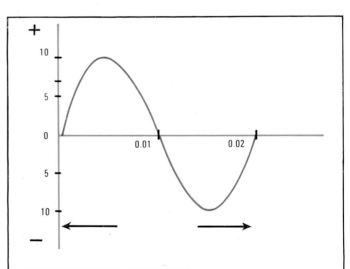

ALTERNATING CURRENT
Alternating current (AC) changes all the time. It builds up to a peak in one direction, drops to zero, builds up to a maximum in the opposite direction and then drops to zero once more. This whole sequence or *cycle* (red line above) repeats itself 60 times every second in the current supplied to our houses. Our electricity has a *frequency* of 60 hertz (60 Hz), a hertz being one cycle per second.

It might seem inconvenient to have electric current that is always changing. In fact, the opposite is true. It is easier to generate alternating current than direct current. And alternating current can easily be changed from one voltage to another, whereas direct current cannot. It is also quite easy to turn AC into DC.

Triodes and Transistors

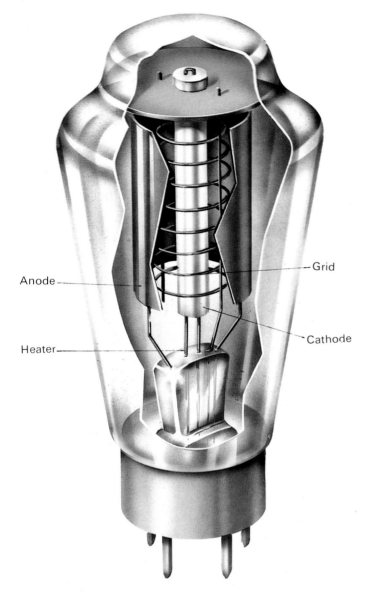

Anode

Heater

Grid

Cathode

The triode valve (above) has a wire mesh, called a grid, between the heated cathode and the anode. A small varying voltage fed to the grid causes larger variations in the electron flow through the valve. The triode amplifies the signals applied to its grid. The symbol below is how a triode valve is represented.

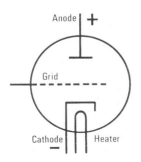

Anode

Grid

Cathode   Heater

In 1947, three scientists working at the Bell Telephone Company's laboratories invented a wonderful new device called the transistor. The transistor could do what the triode valve could do, but it was much smaller, stronger and cheaper.

The triode is a valve that is used to amplify (strengthen) television or radio signals. It is called a triode because it has three main parts inside it (tri means three). As well as the cathode and the anode, it has something called a *grid*. The grid is usually a coil of fine wire or a screen between the cathode and the anode.

When a negative charge is applied to the grid, the electrons from the cathode are pushed back and cannot get through. But if a positive charge is applied to the grid, lots of electrons are pulled from the cathode through the grid to the anode. A strong current passes through the valve.

The triode amplifies because even tiny charges applied to the grid cause big changes in the current flowing through the valve. Weak signals picked up by an antenna in a radio set go to the grid of a triode or some similar kind of valve. These changing weak signals cause big changes in the current flowing through the valve. The valve is an amplifier.

Transistors

Some substances let electricity flow through them easily. They are called *conductors*. Metals are conductors. Other substances don't let electricity pass through them. These are *insulators*. Plastics, rubber and glass are insulators.

But there are some substances that are neither conductors nor insulators. These are called *semiconductors*.

In 1947, a very important discovery was made. Scientists found that by arranging pieces of semiconducting material in the right way, the pieces could do the same jobs as valves. They could amplify small currents, just as a valve could. These little pieces of semiconductor were much smaller than valves, needed much less power to work them, and lasted much much longer. They were called *transistors*. They were made of silicon – a cheap material made mostly of sand.

With transistors it was possible to build smaller and much more reliable radios, television sets and computers. The valve was no longer needed for

these machines. It is still used, however, where high voltages are needed, such as in television, radio and radar transmitters.

To make transistors work, small amounts of other elements called *impurities* had to be added to the silicon. When different impurities are added to two pieces of silicon that are joined together, the whole transistor becomes a better conductor of electricity. But only in one direction. Electrons pass easily from one side to the other, but they cannot get back again. The pieces of silicon behave just like a diode valve. They change AC into DC electricity.

If a sandwich is made of a specially treated piece of silicon between two differently treated pieces of silicon, the device becomes an amplifier. The large current flowing between the two ends of the sandwich can be controlled by very small voltage changes applied to the center of the sandwich. The transistor is working like a very small triode valve.

Smaller and Smaller

At first, transistors were small individual parts, like tiny valves. These became smaller and smaller as time went by until it was discovered that it was not necessary always to sandwich pieces of silicon together to make transistors. By adding different impurities to the same little piece of silicon, scientists found that they could make not only transistors but other kinds of electrical components as well. They could make things called resistors and capacitors too. And, what was most important, they could put them all on the same tiny piece of silicon, jammed together in a very small electrical circuit.

Because all the parts of the circuit can be made together on a single chip of silicon, we call this an *integrated circuit*. The integrated circuit is one of the most important inventions of our century. It has led to the computer age.

Above: An early valve radio set, with speaker and headphones. Below: If a transistor is made of two different pieces of silicon, electrons pass easily from one side to the other, but not back again. When a sandwich is made of a specially treated piece of silicon between two differently treated pieces of silicon, the device becomes an amplifier. The center of the sandwich acts in the same way as the grid in a triode.

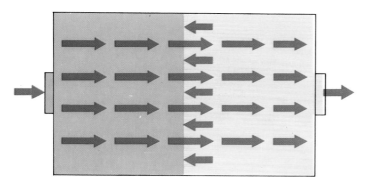

Below: Two ways of representing a transistor.

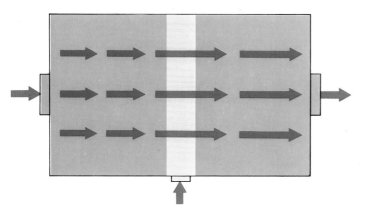

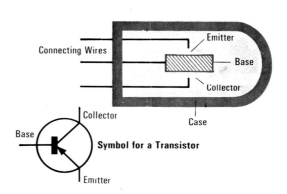

13

Smaller and Smaller

The word "chip" means a small, thin piece of something that has been cut or struck off. Now it also means a tiny piece of the element silicon packed with thousands of electronic parts. Such a chip, $\frac{3}{16}$ inch square, can now be the main part of a computer.

Silicon chips are cheap to buy because hundreds of identical chips can be made at the same time on one thin slice of silicon about 4 inches (10cm) in diameter. But the equipment that makes the chips is very complicated. The workers who make the chips look like surgeons in an operating theater, because the smallest speck of dirt or dust could ruin the whole process.

The design of the circuit to be etched into the chip depends on what it is to be used for – a digital watch, a pocket calculator or a computer. The circuit is first drawn to a large size with the help of a computer. Then it is reduced smaller and smaller by taking photographs of it until the individual parts of the circuit cannot be seen by the human eye. The circuit is then etched into the slice of silicon, layer by layer, by a special process.

There may be as many as 500 tiny chips, each about $\frac{3}{16}$ inch (5mm) square on one slice of silicon. The little chips are then cut apart and sealed into plastic cases. Fine gold wires are attached to the outside connections and they are ready to be used.

The number of microscopic transistors that can be put on a chip measuring $\frac{3}{16}$ inch (5mm) square has increased rapidly year by year. It is now possible to put more than a million of them on a single chip. Each of the million parts does the job that a large glass valve did only a few years ago.

The Microprocessor

The first integrated circuits were made to do particular jobs in certain calculators or computers. This kind of chip is still being made. But in the 1970s scientists began designing integrated circuits that would suit all kinds of calculators, computers and other electronic devices. This magic chip is called the *microprocessor* – a tiny computer only $\frac{3}{16}$ inch (5mm) square. This little chip is now the heart of all the microcomputers.

Below, left to right: Grains of sand magnified many times. Sand is mostly silicon, but the silicon used to make chips has to be very pure. The next picture shows the first stage in making chips. A pure silicon rod about 4 in in diameter is sliced into thin disk-shaped wafers. Hundreds of tiny chips will be made from each slice. The circuits to be etched on the chips are very complex and can be projected on a screen. A designer can make changes by using a light pen. In the next picture, hundreds of identical chips have been etched into the silicon wafer but not yet cut apart. The size can be compared to the watch movement. In the last picture the chip is ready for use. This tiny electronic marvel can do the same job that a whole roomful of tubes could do 20 years ago. The big picture on the right shows what a small part of the chip looks like through a microscope. You can see how complicated it is.

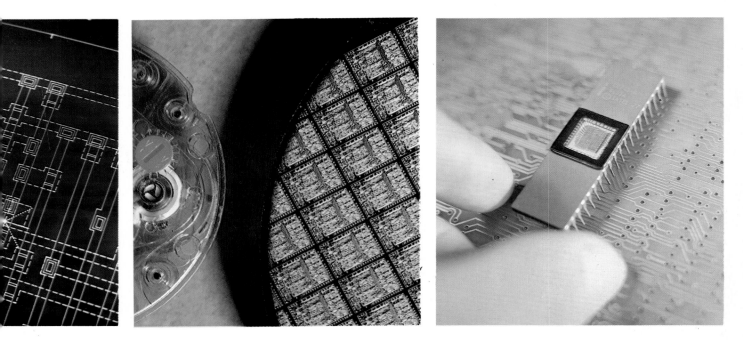

Magic Radio Waves

Heinrich Hertz made electric sparks shoot across a gap between two metal balls. Although he did not know it at the time, he was beginning a story that led to our receiving television pictures from the Moon.

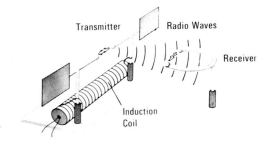

Heinrich Hertz was the first person to make radio waves travel through space. With the simple apparatus above he made them travel from the coil transmitter to the receiver.

To send messages across empty space, television, radio and radar use *electromagnetic waves*. These invisible waves act something like water waves. If you throw a stone into still water, circles of ripples spread out from where the stone hit the water. The ripples get smaller and smaller the further they are from the center. These small water waves are not made up of water that travels outwards. They are only an up-and-down movement of the water. Throw a stick into the circle of wavelets and it will only bob up and down. It won't be carried along by the movement of the waves.

Ripples from the splash soon die away. But the larger the stone the bigger the ripples and the farther they travel. Radio waves travel outward in all directions from the transmitting antenna. The more powerful the waves, the farther they travel through space.

The Story of Radio

Long before radio was invented, one man said that it would be possible to send electromagnetic waves through the air. In 1865, the famous British scientist James Clerk Maxwell said that it could be done, although he didn't know how to do it.

Then, in 1888, the German Heinrich Hertz showed that Maxwell was right. Hertz generated a strong electric current that was able to jump as a spark between two knobs at the end of metal rods.

Each time a spark occurred, electromagnetic waves were sent out. Hertz proved this by holding a metal ring with knobs at each end several feet from the spark. When sparks jumped the gap at the transmitter, sparks also jumped between the knobs of his receiving ring. This was the first time that anyone had sent out radio signals and received them.

Radio waves travel at the same speed as all other electromagnetic waves – light waves, heat waves and X-rays. This speed is the fastest that we know of – 186,282 miles (299,792 km) per second.

Guglielmo Marconi

Other scientists were fascinated by the idea of sending messages from place to place without using wires. Among these scientists was the Italian Guglielmo Marconi. He saw the enormous possibilities of the new "wireless" and by 1901 he had succeeded in sending spark signals across the Atlantic from Cornwall to Newfoundland.

But Marconi's spark transmitter could only send out a high-pitched buzz. This buzz was interrupted to form the dots and dashes of the Morse Code.

The sound of the human voice and music could not be transmitted successfully until the valve was invented. To carry speech or music, radio waves have to be continuous, not short bursts of sparks.

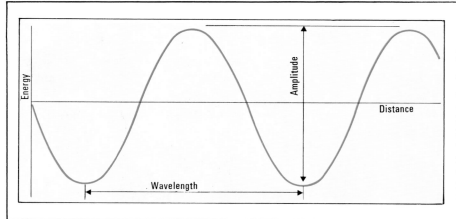

RADIO WAVES

Radio waves travel at the speed of light – 186,282 miles (299,792 km) per second. This speed never changes. The length of the waves varies between less than $\frac{4}{100}$ inch (1mm) to over 20 miles (30 km). The height of a wave is called its *amplitude*; the higher the amplitude, the more powerful the wave. The frequency of waves is the number of waves that pass a certain point every second. Millions of radio waves can pass in a second. The higher the frequency, the shorter the wavelength.

Guglielmo Marconi, an Italian, was the most famous of the radio pioneers.

How Does Radio Work?

In a broadcasting studio, someone speaks into a microphone. The microphone turns the sound waves coming from the speaker's voice into an electric current that varies as the speaker's voice varies. But this current is much too weak to broadcast. It is amplified by transistors to become a stronger varying electric current. This current is called the *audio frequency* current. It goes along wires to the broadcasting transmitter.

At the transmitter, a *carrier wave* is produced. This wave is made to oscillate (vibrate) at a fixed frequency by a special quartz crystal.

The audio frequency signals are then joined up with the carrier wave to make a carrier wave that varies as the audio frequency varies. When this occurs, we say that the carrier wave is *modulated*. The modulated carrier wave is amplified and fed to the transmitter antenna. There it makes the radio waves that travel out into space. This kind of modulation is called *amplitude modulation* or AM.

The other way of joining the audio frequency to the carrier wave is called *frequency modulation* or FM. As the name suggests, the frequency of the carrier wave changes as the audio frequency carrying the speaker's voice changes. When the signal from the microphone is strong, the carrier wave frequency varies a lot – the waves are jammed together. When the signal from the microphone is weak, the carrier wave frequency changes much less – the waves are spread apart. But the height of the carrier wave always stays the same. The frequencies of FM radio stations are much higher than those of AM stations. The VHF waveband stations on our radio sets are frequency modulated.

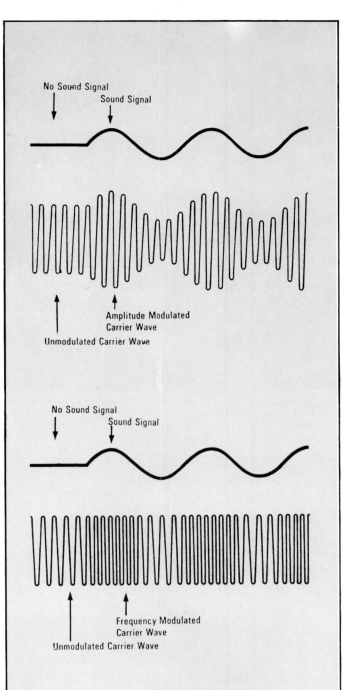

MODULATING THE RADIO WAVES

In amplitude modulation (AM), sound is added to the carrier wave by changing its amplitude (height). When the signal from the microphone is strong, the amplitude of the carrier wave increases. When the signal is weak, the amplitude is small, as shown above.

In frequency modulation (FM), when signals from the microphone are strong, the frequency of the carrier wave increases. When the signal is weak, the frequency changes less. The height (amplitude) of the carrier wave does not vary, as shown above. The stations on the VHF band of our radios are frequency modulated. Frequency modulation cuts out interference from other electrical equipment and from thunderstorms.

Radio Waves Around the World

Radio waves, like light waves and heat waves, are electromagnetic. Electromagnetic waves are very mysterious. We can do all kinds of clever things with them – we can make them light and heat our homes, give us radio and television. But no one knows exactly what they are.

Unlike sound waves, radio waves can travel anywhere, whether there is air or not. We have listened to astronauts on the Moon talking by radio to Earth. Space probes on their way to the outer planets are still controlled by radio signals.

But in some ways it is easier to send radio signals to the Moon than it is to send them to the other side of the Earth. Radio waves travel in straight lines but cannot go through the Earth. Ordinary short waves can be sent round the world by bouncing them up and down off a layer of electrically charged air about 100 miles (150 km) above the Earth.

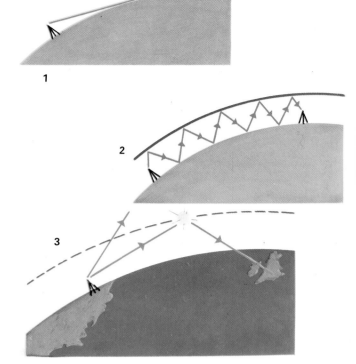

Above: Radio waves travel in straight lines. Some waves go along the ground, but they cannot be used over long distances because of the curve of the Earth (1). Other waves shoot upward until they hit a band of the atmosphere called the ionosphere. From this they bounce back to Earth. They can bounce up and down between Earth and the ionosphere all the way round the Earth (2). But not all radio waves bounce back from the ionosphere. Some very short waves such as those used for television go straight through and disappear into space. If we want to send television pictures across the Atlantic, we have to bounce them back to Earth from a special satellite over the ocean (3).

Below: As time goes by, communications satellites will become bigger and more powerful. It will then be possible to relay television broadcasts from any part of the world directly to our television antennas. This will cut out the need for expensive ground stations.

Below right: The antenna display of a satellite communications ground station.

Opposite page: Weather satellites like this radio down information that is used by our weather forecasters.

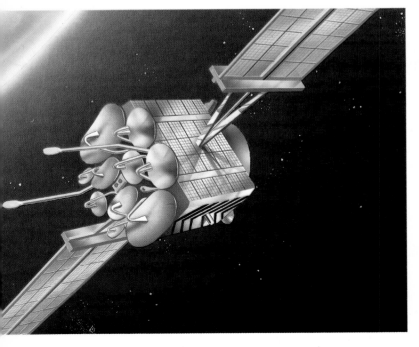

Audio frequency waves in the air are those that can be heard by the human ear. They range in frequency from about 20 to 20,000 hertz. (A hertz, usually abbreviated as Hz, is one complete cycle per second.) Low frequency sounds are low-pitched, high frequencies are high-pitched. Each musical note has its own vibration rate. The lowest note on a piano has a frequency of 27 Hz. Our ability to hear high-pitched sounds grows less as we get older. Children can hear sounds higher than 20,000 Hz, and dogs can hear even higher.

If we want to find the wavelength of any sound or radio wave we use the formula $\lambda = v/f$, λ is the wavelength in meters, v is the velocity (speed) of the waves in meters per second, and f is the frequency of the vibrations in hertz (cycles per second). Sound travels through air at a speed of about 330 meters (1080ft) per second (its velocity).

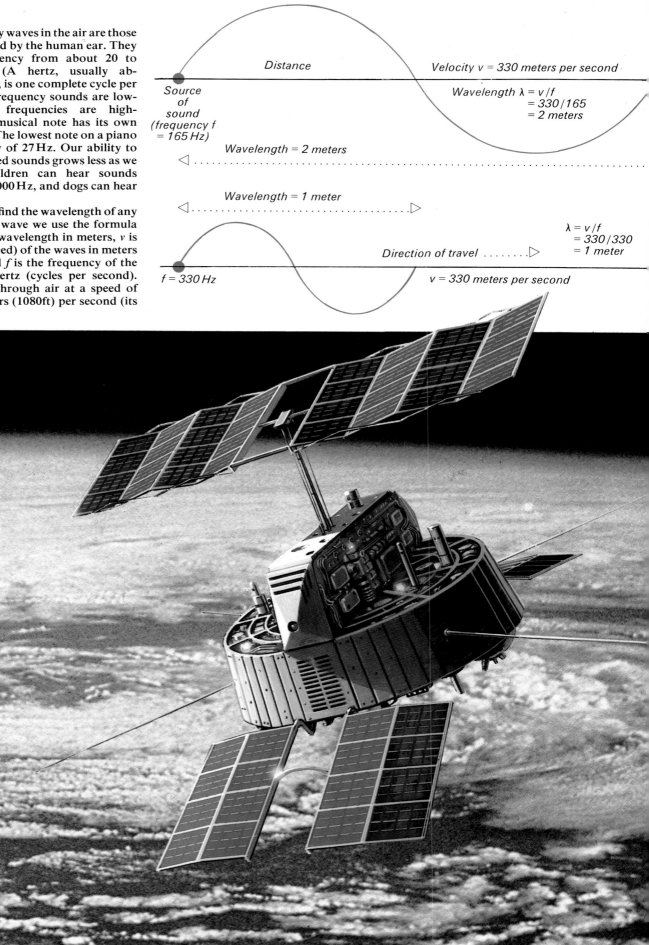

Distance

Velocity v = 330 meters per second

Source of sound (frequency f = 165 Hz)

Wavelength $\lambda = v/f$
= 330/165
= 2 meters

Wavelength = 2 meters

Wavelength = 1 meter

Direction of travel

$\lambda = v/f$
= 330/330
= 1 meter

f = 330 Hz

v = 330 meters per second

Sound from Radio Waves

As you read this, unseen radio waves are passing right through you at the speed of light. These waves come from radio stations all over the world and even from outer space. Our radio sets can trap these waves and turn them into sounds of speech and music.

Radio waves from the transmitter pass through most things, including the walls of our houses and ourselves. Radio waves of many different frequencies are always all around us although we don't know they are there.

Some of the waves strike the antenna in our radio. This antenna may be a metal rod or coils of wire inside the set. As the waves strike the antenna they produce tiny electric currents in the metal.

When you tune into a particular radio station by turning the tuning knob, you are adjusting a tuning circuit in the set. When you turn the knob, a variable capacitor tunes the circuit to the frequency of the radio station you want to hear. Each station broadcasts on a different carrier wave frequency that is carefully controlled.

The tuning circuit allows waves of the frequency you want to pass through. These waves are then amplified by transistors. But there are still a few unwanted frequencies left in the signal – frequencies from other stations. The carrier wave is changed to an *intermediate* frequency by mixing it with waves from a small oscillator in the set. Then these intermediate frequency signals are passed through a tuned circuit that allows only the intermediate frequency through.

Now the radio set has gotten rid of all unwanted frequencies. The frequency we need is amplified

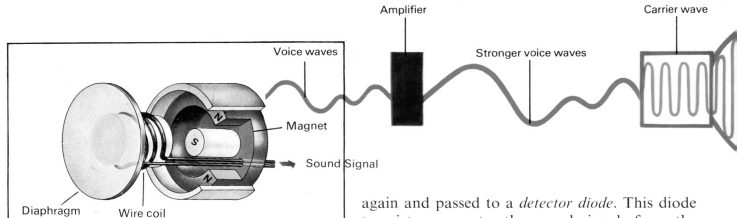

Amplifier

Carrier wave

Voice waves

Stronger voice waves

Magnet

Sound Signal

Diaphragm   Wire coil

SOUND INTO ELECTRICITY

Any sound, whether it comes from someone speaking, an explosion or a large orchestra, causes the air to vibrate. These air vibrations can be made to work a microphone. The one shown here is a *moving coil microphone*.

When sound waves hit the flat diaphragm they make it vibrate at the same rate as the sound waves. A coil of wire is attached to the diaphragm. As the diaphragm vibrates, so does the coil.

Around the coil is a strong magnet. When a coil of wire vibrates close to a magnet, electric currents are set up in the coil. The electric current in the coil varies as the sound waves of the voice or the instrument. This tiny current travels through wires connected to the coil and goes off to be amplified by transistors. This is called the *audio frequency* current. The word "audio" comes from the Latin word for "hear."

again and passed to a *detector diode*. This diode transistor separates the sound signals from the carrier waves. Only the sound signals are wanted now.

The sound signals are amplified until they are strong enough to work a loudspeaker. (By turning up the volume control on your set you can amplify them to the strength you want.)

All this complicated process – from the moment someone speaks into a microphone in the broadcasting studio to your hearing the voice coming from your loudspeaker – occurs in a flash. In fact, it takes longer for the sound waves to travel the few feet from the loudspeaker to your ears than it takes the waves to travel from the transmitting antenna to your loudspeaker, perhaps hundreds of miles apart.

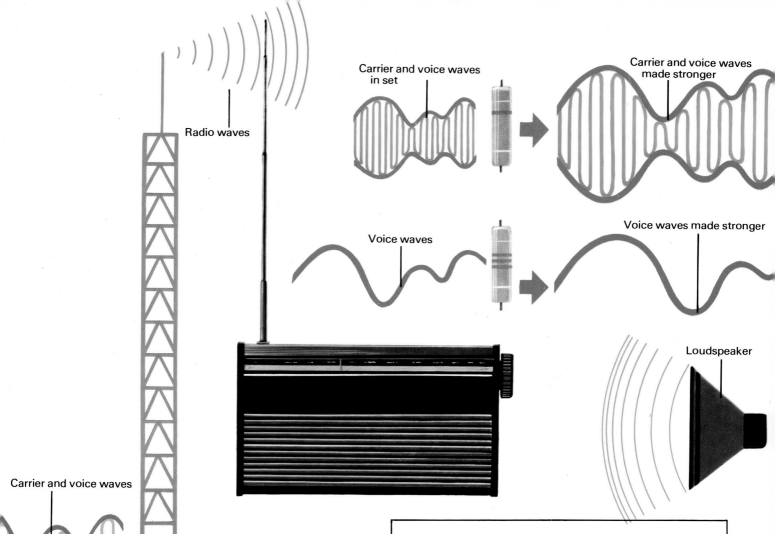

Radio waves

Carrier and voice waves
in set

Carrier and voice waves
made stronger

Voice waves

Voice waves made stronger

Loudspeaker

Carrier and voice waves

ELECTRICITY INTO SOUND

Loudspeakers work rather like microphones in reverse. The microphone turns sound waves into electric currents. The loudspeaker turns electric currents into sound. Sound wave electric currents come from the final amplifier in the radio and travel around the coil in the loudspeaker. This changing current makes the coil vibrate inside its magnet. The speaker's stiff paper cone is attached to the coil, so the cone vibrates at the same speed. This vibration of the cone makes sound waves in the air which travel out to our ears. We hear the speaker's voice or the musical instrument just as it sounded in the studio.

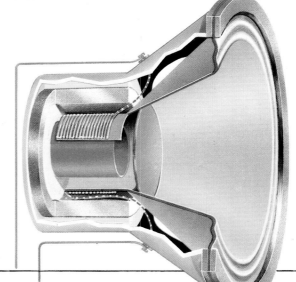

S   N

MAGNETS AND ELECTRICITY

The loudspeakers and microphones shown on these pages work because electricity and magnetism go hand in hand. Every magnet (above) has a magnetic field all around it. If a wire is moved in this field, an electric current is created in the wire.

If we pass an electric current through a coil of wire (below) and have an iron rod inside the coil, a powerful magnet is formed. This is called an *electromagnet*.

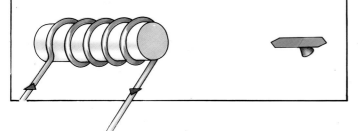

Turning Pictures into Waves

In 1939, NBC began the first regular TV broadcasts in the U.S. Ten years later, the boom was well underway: a million American homes had TV sets. Today, there are over 155 million sets in the U.S. and over 470 million receivers across the globe. Television is part of people's lives the world over.

In television, light from objects in the studio is changed into electric currents in the television camera. These electric currents are broadcast by the transmitter as radio waves. When the broadcast waves reach your television set, they are changed back into electric currents and then into pictures in your TV tube.

The Television Camera

When we look at something, our eyes are seeing light reflected from whatever we are looking at. Nearly everything reflects light, but things we see as "dark" reflect very little.

When a TV camera is pointed at something, light from the object is focused by the camera's lens onto a *target plate* inside the camera. The target plate is coated with a special chemical that shoots out electrons when light hits it. The more light that shines on any part of the target plate, the more electrons are given out by that part.

We have seen that electrons carry a small negative electric charge. So the parts of the target plate that have given off electrons are left with a *positive* charge. The parts that have given off a lot of electrons have a strong positive charge. The parts that have given off few electrons have a weak positive charge. This means that the target plate now carries an "electrical picture" of whatever the TV camera is pointing at.

The Electron Gun

At the far end of the camera tube is something called an *electron gun*. This gun shoots out a stream of electrons which travels over the target plate in much the same way we read the page of a book, except the beam skips every other line. The beam of electrons starts at the top left-hand corner of the target plate, then moves from left to right across the plate, returns rapidly to the left again and scans the third line, fifth line and so on. When the beam reaches the bottom of the electrical picture on the target plate it returns to the top and starts all over again, this time scanning even-numbered lines.

The electron beam reads 525 lines from top to bottom. It does this 30 times a second.

Reading the Picture

As the electron beam travels over the electrical picture on the target plate it gives lots of electrons to the places that are highly positive (positives and negatives attract each other), and fewer electrons to places that are not so positive.

As the electron beam travels back down the camera tube it therefore carries with it the electrical picture from the target plate. This stream of returning electrons becomes a varying electric current that goes out of the TV camera along a cable. The scene in the studio has been turned into an electric current that can be transmitted on radio waves.

The Color Television Camera

The explanation above applies to a black and white television camera. In color cameras there are usually three tubes inside instead of one.

White light is made up of all the colors of the rainbow, but by mixing the three primary colors of light, red, green and blue, we can make almost any color we want. Color cameras are made to distinguish these colors and separate them from each other.

Light from the scene in the studio goes through the camera's lens system and strikes a special mirror. This is called a *dichroic* mirror. It reflects blue light on to an ordinary mirror, which shines the blue light through a lens and onto the target plate of one of the three tubes.

The red and green light goes straight through the blue mirror to another dichroic mirror. This mirror lets the green light go through straight on to the green target plate. The red light is reflected to another ordinary mirror and onto the red target plate.

The light from the studio scene has now been split up into three colors. In each of the camera tubes electron beams scan the target plates, just as in a black and white tube. So we have three lots of electric currents going out to the transmitting station.

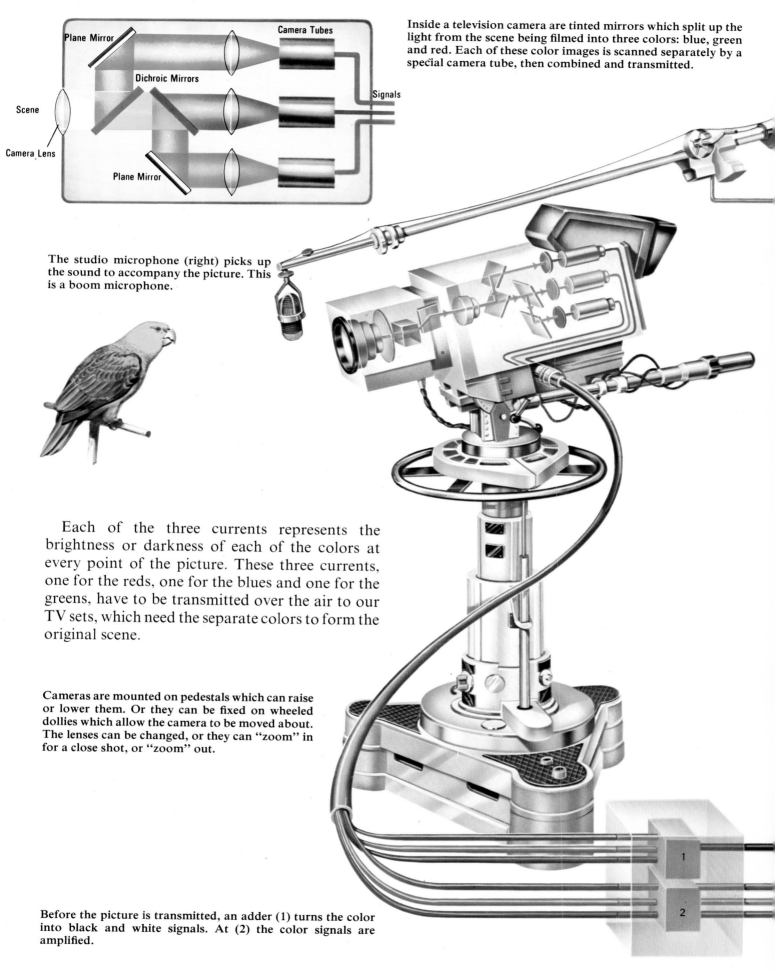

Plane Mirror

Camera Tubes

Dichroic Mirrors

Scene

Camera Lens

Plane Mirror

Signals

Inside a television camera are tinted mirrors which split up the light from the scene being filmed into three colors: blue, green and red. Each of these color images is scanned separately by a special camera tube, then combined and transmitted.

The studio microphone (right) picks up the sound to accompany the picture. This is a boom microphone.

Each of the three currents represents the brightness or darkness of each of the colors at every point of the picture. These three currents, one for the reds, one for the blues and one for the greens, have to be transmitted over the air to our TV sets, which need the separate colors to form the original scene.

Cameras are mounted on pedestals which can raise or lower them. Or they can be fixed on wheeled dollies which allow the camera to be moved about. The lenses can be changed, or they can "zoom" in for a close shot, or "zoom" out.

Before the picture is transmitted, an adder (1) turns the color into black and white signals. At (2) the color signals are amplified.

Unscrambling the Pictures

Television pictures travel through space on radio waves. When they reach our TV sets, the pictures are taken from the waves and sorted into their correct colors. We see the scene in the television studio the moment it happens because radio waves travel at the speed of light.

The electric signals from the TV camera are sent along cables to the transmitter. So are the sound waves from the microphone. The three color signals and the sound signal are all combined on radio carrier waves and transmitted just like sound waves.

Sending TV pictures on radio waves is more difficult than sending sound alone. The bandwidth needed for TV transmission is much greater – in fact, over 300 times as great. This is because of the separate sound signals and the separate colors. For this reason, TV transmission usually takes place on VHF (very high frequency) or UHF (ultra high frequency) waves.

For simplicity, white light is usually considered to be made up of just three colors – red, green and blue. These are the primary colors of light and they can be mixed to give almost any other color.

Radio waves carrying TV signals cannot travel very far because of their very high frequency. In fact, they cannot usually travel more than about 60 miles (100 km). The waves travel in a straight line from the transmitting antenna and do not follow the curve of the Earth. They can only go as far as the horizon. So TV antennas are placed as high as possible. Mountains block the waves. This

Inside your television set, between the electron gun and the screen, is the shadow mask. This mask has thousands of tiny holes, and the combined red, blue and green signals go through each hole together and hit the screen. The screen is covered with tiny dots that light up to make the picture.

is why people living in mountainous areas have difficulty in receiving good TV pictures.

Long-distance TV

To send television signals over long distances, the waves can be picked up by relay stations, amplified and passed on to the next station. Or the signals can be sent along *coaxial cables.* These are special cables that consist of a copper tube with a copper wire inside. The wire is held away from the tube by insulators so the wire and tube don't touch. The job of the tube is to shield the signals passing along the wire from outside electrical interference. It also helps to prevent the signals from losing their strength. The antenna lead to your TV set is coaxial.

Long-distance TV signals are also sent by satellite. This is the best way of broadcasting over very long distances. The radio waves carrying the TV signals are sent up to a satellite positioned several thousand miles above the earth. The satellite receives the signals and beams them back to a special "dish" antenna in the receiving country. In this way TV signals are broadcast across the Atlantic.

TV signals can also be sent along fiber optic cables. A laser beam is used to carry the signals along the special glass cable. Each fiber optic cable using laser light can carry hundreds of TV channels at a time.

Inside Your TV Set

When the radio waves carrying the TV signals strike your television antenna, they are changed to small varying electric currents that travel down a cable to the antenna socket in your set. Then, in a flash, all sorts of things happen to the tiny currents.

First of all, they pass through a tuner which only allows waves through that are of the frequency of the TV program you want. You probably have push buttons on your set to choose which channel's signals you require.

Then the signals are amplified, rectified (changed from AC to DC), and the sound signal is separated from the picture signals. The three color picture signals are also separated from each other and go to the picture tube in your set.

The picture tube works very much like the tube in the TV camera. But it works the other way around. The tube has three electron guns, one for each of the three primary colors. The red, blue and green signals are fed to these guns, which fire

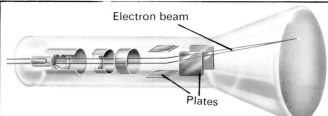

Electron beam

Plates

CATHODE RAY TUBES

The picture tube in your TV set is a *cathode ray tube.* These tubes are used for other purposes such as radar screens and *oscilloscopes.* Oscilloscopes are tubes which display electric signals in graph form on a screen. The cathode ray tube (CRT) is a glass tube which has had the air pumped out of it. Inside, an electron gun shoots a beam of electrons towards the screen at the far end. The screen is *fluorescent* – it glows when electrons hit it.

The electron beams must be made to scan the whole screen. In the oscilloscope shown above, plates change the angle of the beam depending on how much electric current is fed into them. One set of plates makes the beam go up and down, the other pair make it go across the screen.

streams of electrons at the screen which fills the wide end of the tube. (This is the screen that you look at.) The screen is coated on the inside with tiny dots of a chemical that glows red, blue or green, depending on which electron gun is shooting its electron beam at it.

Between the electron gun and the screen is a plate called a *shadow mask.* This mask has thousands of tiny holes. The combined red, blue and green signals go through each hole together and hit the screen.

The picture signals control how many electrons are leaving the guns at any moment. A strong beam of electrons from the red gun makes a strong red spot on the screen. A weak electron beam from the green gun makes a weak green spot. All the beams are focused on the same area at the same time. The beams move across the screen, line by line, just as the beams in the TV camera do.

If you look closely at your TV screen when the set is switched on you will see that the picture is made up of hundreds of horizontal lines. In the U.S. there are 525 of these lines. But in most of the world's TV sets there are 625 lines. Along these lines are the tiny color dots that make up our picture. As the electron beams flash across the screen, the tiny red, blue and green dots light up and fade so quickly that our eyes are quite unaware of them. All we see is the overall color picture, very like the scene in front of the camera in the TV studio.

In the newest TV tubes, colored stripes rather than dots are used.

Recording Sound on Tape

Before we find out how television pictures are recorded on tape, we will have a look at sound recording.

A tape recorder is an electronic machine that records sound on a special kind of tape. Most tape recorders can also play back the sound recorded.

The tape on which recordings are made is a thin plastic ribbon. It is coated on one side with millions of tiny, invisible particles of a substance that is easily magnetized – usually iron oxide. When the tape comes close to a magnet, all these tiny particles swing round like compass needles. But, unlike compass needles, when the magnet is taken away, the particles remain pointing in their new direction. In blank tape that has not been recorded on, the particles all point in different directions. The tape has no overall magnetization.

Putting Sound on Tape

When sound signals come from a microphone they can be changed into small electric currents. The signals in a radio receiver are already in this form.

These currents vary as the original sounds of someone speaking or making music vary.

The tiny currents are amplified before going to the *recording head* of the tape recorder. The recording head is an electromagnet – a piece of iron with a coil of wire around it. When electric current goes through the coil, a magnetic field appears around the iron. The iron is shaped like an open ring, with a tiny gap in the ring where the strongest magnetic field occurs.

The sound signal current goes through the magnet's coils, making the magnetic field vary as the sound signals vary. Then, when the tape passes across the gap at the front of the recording head, the particles of iron oxide in the tape are magnetized by the magnetic field. A very strong signal through the head will pull most of the particles on the passing tape so that they point in the same direction. The tape has a strong magnetic pattern. Weaker signals passing through the recording head bring few particles into line. The tape has a weaker magnetic pattern. In this way, every variation of the signal passing through the recording head is recorded on the tape as it passes.

In a tape recorder, sounds are recorded as a magnetized pattern on tape. The tape is made of plastic and has a coating of magnetic iron oxide on one side. As the capstan rotates, it pulls the tape past tape heads. The erase head wipes out any existing recording on the tape. The record head causes a varying current that corresponds to the sound to be recorded. This magnetizes the tape. A signal is induced in the playback head when the tape passes it. This signal can be amplified and heard as a copy of the original sound.

This is how a professional recorder works. Our home recorders have only two heads – an erase head and a record/playback head.

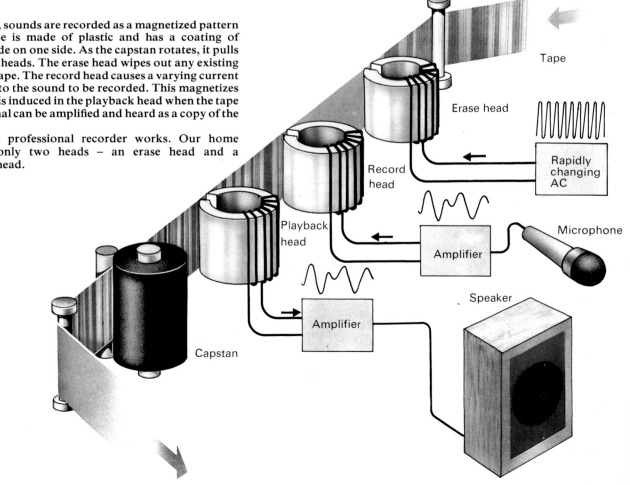

Tape

Erase head

Rapidly changing AC

Record head

Microphone

Amplifier

Playback head

Speaker

Amplifier

Capstan

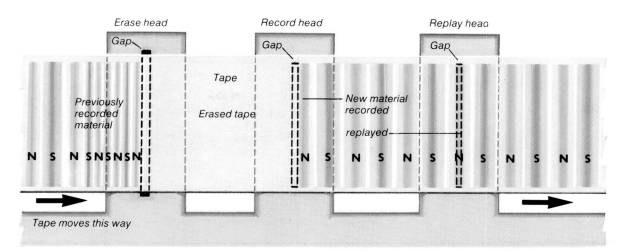

Gap

Gap

Gap

Tape

Previously
recorded
material

Erased tape

New material
recorded

replayed

N   S   N   SNSNSN   N   S   N   S   N   S   N   S   N   S   N   S

Tape moves this way

There has to be a separate electromagnet for each track on the tape. If stereo sound is being recorded, there have to be two separate electromagnets.

To get the very best quality recordings, a high tape speed is needed. This is why professional recorders as used in studios usually run at a speed of 15 inches (38 cm) per second. However, for most of us, the ordinary cassette gives good enough quality. You merely push it into the machine, and it is ready for use. Cassettes run at a speed of only $1\frac{7}{8}$ inches (4.8 cm) per second and use thin tape so that as much as possible can be fitted into the case. Most cassettes have a total running time of 60 or 90 minutes, although 120 minutes is possible with extra-thin tape.

The cassette has two reels or spools – a feed spool and a take-up spool. The spool from which the tape is unwinding is the feed spool. The spools can be driven in either direction so that the tape can be wound either way.

The tape, which is only 1.15 inches (3.8 mm) wide, usually has two pairs of stereo tracks. One pair is used when the tape goes in one direction. Then the tape is turned over and the other pair is used.

Playing Back the Tape

When the tape is being played back it is pulled across the electromagnet by a capstan (a small, rotating shaft) driven by a small electric motor. (This same drive was used in the recording process.) As the tape passes the gap in the magnet, the magnetic pattern that has been fixed on the tape makes varying electric currents in the electromagnet's coils. These varying currents are amplified and go to the loudspeaker. The loudspeaker turns them into sound waves that we can hear.

Another way of showing how the previously recorded pattern is erased by the first head; how new sound is recorded by the record head, leaving a magnetized pattern on the tape. This pattern produces a sound signal in the replay head.

Getting Rid of the Recording

The sound signals can be erased from a tape by running the tape past an *erase head*. The erase head has a circuit which has a rapidly changing alternating current passing through it. This changing current makes a changing magnetic field which destroys any magnetic pattern on the tape. The tape is left unmagnetized over all.

It is not necessary, however, to specially erase a tape if you want to make a new recording on it. On most cassette recorders the erase head comes on automatically to wipe the tape clean of sound pattern before it reaches the recording head.

A tape recorder. It uses tape 0.15 inch wide and runs at a speed of $1\frac{7}{8}$ inch per second. When the machine is switched to replay or record, the heads and the pressure roller move toward the cassette. The tape is pulled past the heads by the capstan. The right-hand spool turns gently to take up the tape.

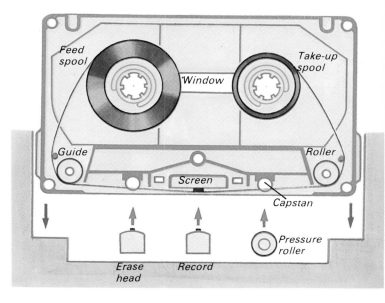

Feed
spool

Window

Take-up
spool

Guide

Screen

Roller

Capstan

Pressure
roller

Erase
head

Record

Video

The broadcasting companies have been using video recording to make their TV programs since the late 1950s. Now we have video cassette recorders that we can use in our own homes. Pictures and sound are stored on the video tape, to be played back at any time we want to.

When we hear the word "video" we tend to think of home video recorders. But only a few years ago there were no such things. Video recording was invented to help television producers. Before it was invented, TV programs had either to go out live or be shot on ordinary film, which was expensive. Producers wanted to be able to reshoot bits of programs that went wrong. And, of course, programs that went out live and were not on film were lost for ever.

Nowadays, nearly all television programs are recorded on video tape.

Recording Pictures on Tape

Scientists tried for many years to find a successful way of recording pictures on tape. It was much more difficult to record pictures than it was to record sound. As we have seen on previous pages, much more information has to be sent out with picture signals than with sound signals. This is also the case with tape recording. To record pictures with any detail, the area of tape used has to be much greater than with sound. And the speed of the tape had to be much higher – up to 240 inches

(600 cm) per second, which is very fast indeed. We can understand this problem when we think that in sound recording, wave frequencies from 20 to 20,000 hertz have to be recorded on the tape. In video, the range of frequencies needed is about 5 *million* hertz. Much, much more information has to be put on the tape.

In 1956, the Ampex Corporation produced a system for recording pictures on magnetic tape. But the machinery was very bulky and expensive. It was meant to be used by television companies, not in the home. The tape in this system was 2 inches (5 cm) wide, but the speed of the tape had now been reduced to 15 inches (38 centimeters) a second.

Then, in 1972, the first video cassette recorders appeared. With these, the tape was in spools in a plastic container, just like an ordinary sound cassette. The video recorder could now be used in the home.

Unfortunately, there are three different systems of video recorders on sale. Although each system has more or less the same method of recording the pictures, it is not possible to use a tape recorded on one machine to play back on any of the other machines.

The Video Tapes

Modern home video tapes are only $\frac{1}{2}$-inch wide, and they do not travel very fast. But there are two recording heads on a drum $2\frac{1}{2}$ to 3 inches (6.5 to 7.5 cm) in diameter. This drum goes around very fast, so that the recording heads whiz past the tape as it goes round. All this very complicated movement is called *helical scanning*.

As the recording heads whiz past the tape, the electrical currents carrying the picture are

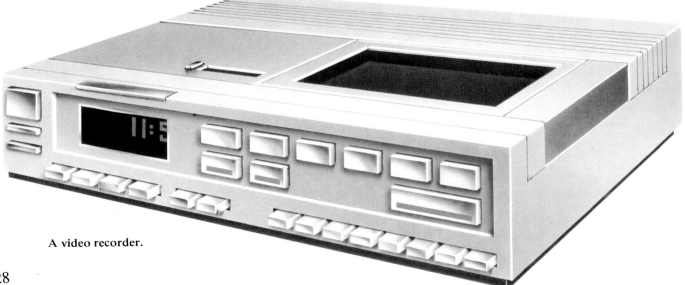

A video recorder.

recorded on the tape, more or less as sound is recorded on sound tape.

At the same time, another fixed recording head puts the sound signals on part of the same tape.

At the bottom of most tapes is another track called the *control track*. This track keeps the speed right.

How Home Video is Used

Most people who have home video recorders use them to record TV programs that are broadcast when they are not at home. Or the program from one TV channel can be recorded while we watch the program on another channel. It is also possible to rent or buy films that have been pre-recorded on cassette.

When a video recorder is being used, the lead from the TV antenna is plugged into the antenna socket at the back of the video. Another lead from the video plugs into the antenna socket of the TV set.

When a television program is being recorded, the signals from the TV antenna go into the video recorder and are turned into magnetized tape. The TV does not even have to be switched on for this to happen. The recorded program can then be played back through the TV set at any time.

In order for the viewer to watch a show while it is being broadcast, signals merely go through the video recorder to the TV set. The program can also be recorded as it is being viewed.

Videos have timers which can be set in advance to record programs that start at a certain time on a certain TV channel. The amount of time ahead that a machine can be set to record varies from 12 hours to about 3 months. Some videos will even record programs on different channels at different times ahead.

Video Disks

Video disks look something like ordinary records. They play back very good quality pictures and sound, but so far they cannot be used for home recording. Video disks are merely prerecorded video records. They are much cheaper to make and buy than video tapes.

Like video tape systems, there are several different systems of video disks. Each system has a different kind of disk that cannot be played on other machines.

One video disk system is worked by laser beams. In this system the picture is recorded on a disk as

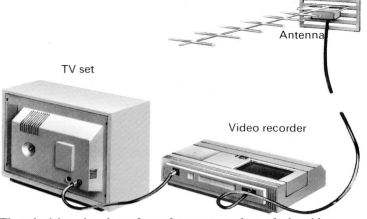

The television signals go from the antenna, through the video recorder to the antenna socket of the TV set. When a program has been recorded, it can be played back through the TV set at any time.

small pits on the smooth surface. The pits are so small they can only be seen through a microscope. In playing the disk, no needle or anything at all touches it. The pits are read by a very fine laser beam and the beam is reflected back as a beam of varying strength. This varying beam is turned into a picture signal which is fed into the TV set and appears on the screen.

Video disks spin very quickly – 1500 revolutions a minute compared to the $33\frac{1}{3}$ revolutions of the ordinary LP.

Video cameras have become smaller and lighter. The girl is carrying a portable video recorder over her shoulder.

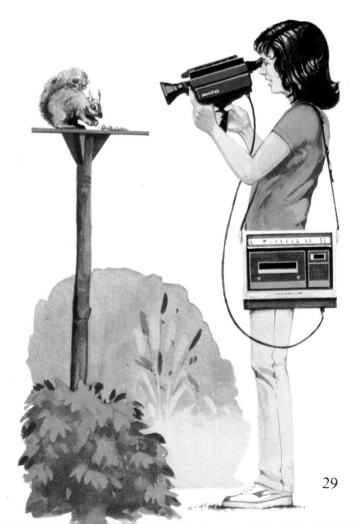

29

Finding Things in the Dark

Since it was first used in World War II, radar has been improved to the point that the positions and speeds of targets moving at very high speeds can be recorded to within a few yards. In fact, the exact position of a tiny fly can be plotted at a distance of over a mile!

You have probably stood in some place where you are surrounded by cliffs or walls and made echoes by shouting and hearing your voice coming back to you. The sound of your voice hits some surface and bounces back. Radar works very much like this. A radar set sends out a signal that hits something such as an aircraft and bounces back. The returning signal tells us in which direction the aircraft is going and how far away it is.

How Does it Work?

A radar set sends out microwaves. We will see in the next two pages that these are a special kind of radio wave with very short wavelengths between 0.04 inches (1mm) and 12 inches (30cm) – frequencies between 300 GHz and 1 GHz. Most radars use wavelengths between 1 and 10 inches (3 and 25cm). Microwaves can be sent out in narrow beams more easily than longer radio waves.

The radar transmitter sends out from its antenna a stream of short bursts or pulses of radio waves. Each pulse lasts for only a few millionths of a second, and there may be more than 10,000 pulses per second. The pulses are separated by a time interval longer than it takes for the radio waves of one pulse to travel to any object and back again. In other words, the radio waves from one pulse travel out to the aircraft or whatever they are aimed at and back again to the radar antenna before the next pulse shoots out.

Finding the Distance

Almost any object in the path of the beam of radar waves reflects back a small part of the beam. So a stream of short pulses arrives back at the radar receiver. We know that all radio waves travel at a speed of about 186,000 miles per second (300,000 kilometers per second). So if a pulse goes out and is reflected back in 1/1000 second, its round trip must have been 186 miles (300km). The target which reflected back the pulse must have been half that distance away – 93 miles (150km). Split-second calculations to find the distance of the target are done automatically by the radar receiver.

Finding the Direction

The direction of a target is found by rotating the radar antenna, thus rotating the beam of radar waves. This beam is something like the beam of a searchlight, so when an echo comes back from a particular direction, the radar operator knows that there must be something in that direction.

How We See the Signals

The very weak signals reflected back from the target are picked up by the same antenna that sent

Today's naval vessels bristle with radar equipment, used to aim missiles at other ships and aircraft.

This Boeing AWACS (Airborne Warning and Control System) aircraft is one of many that patrol the skies day and night to detect enemy aircraft movements. These planes are a mass of radar equipment.

out the strong pulses. These weak signals are fed down a waveguide to the radar receiver. They are amplified before being passed to the display unit. This display unit has a cathode ray tube about 12 to 14 inches (30 to 40cm) in diameter.

Unlike TV tubes, in radar display tubes the

How radar works. The receive/transmit device switches very rapidly between the transmitter and the receiver. The antenna sends out a burst of radio waves each time it is joined to the transmitter. The signals are reflected back from the aircraft to the antenna and passed to the receiver. The receiver amplifies the reflected signals and they are displayed on a screen. Screens can show the range and direction of the aircraft.

beam of electrons travels from the center of the screen to the edge. This beam of electrons goes round the center of the screen at the same speed as the antenna outside. It leaves a *trace* (a thin line of light) on the screen. When an echo is received, it brightens the trace by a "blip" at a point which shows by its distance from the center of the screen how far away the object is. The angle of the trace at that point shows the direction (bearing) of the target. The tube has a coating of fluorescent material. As the trace goes around, the echoes remain as lights on the screen for a short time. So a complete picture of the "scene" observed by the radar waves is built up on the screen.

Uses of Radar

Radar is being used more and more to do all kinds of jobs. A complex international radar system guides aircraft in every part of the world and helps them to land in bad visibility. It is also used to guide ships at sea and in narrow channels.

The armed forces use it to find targets and aim guns and missiles.

The police use it in speed traps to catch vehicles traveling too fast.

It has also been used to track spacecraft and by astronauts in landing on the Moon.

The word radar is short for **R**adio **D**etection **A**nd **R**anging.

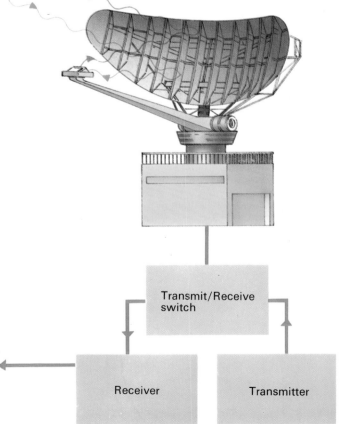

Transmit/Receive switch

Receiver

Transmitter

31

All Kinds of Waves

All radio waves travel in straight lines, but how far they can travel depends very much on how long or short they are.

The whole universe is full of waves. A few of these waves we can detect by our senses. We can see visible light waves. We can feel heat waves. Other waves in the spectrum are radio waves, infra-red waves, ultra-violet waves and X-rays. They all travel at the speed of light, but they have very different frequencies (different wavelengths), and these different wavelengths make them behave in different ways.

The wavelength of electromagnetic waves can

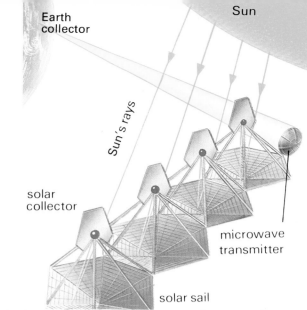

In the future, satellites may harness solar power for use on Earth. Huge satellites, many miles across, will be needed to collect enough energy. They may be made up of solar cells which turn the Sun's energy into electricity, or they may be umbrella-like reflectors. These concentrate sunlight into receivers in which liquid boils to drive generators. The electricity could be beamed down to Earth as microwaves (see diagram).

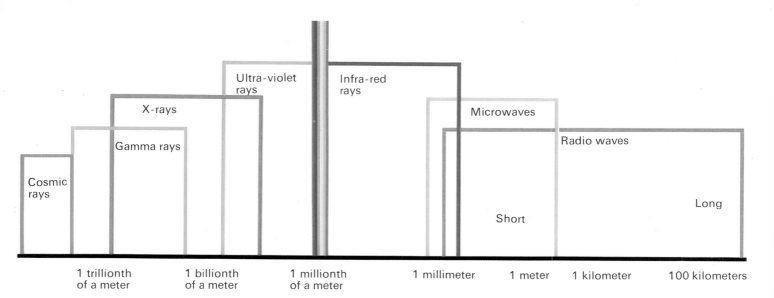

Cosmic rays	Gamma rays	X-rays	Ultra-violet rays	Infra-red rays	Microwaves	Radio waves

| 1 trillionth of a meter | 1 billionth of a meter | 1 millionth of a meter | 1 millimeter | 1 meter | 1 kilometer | 100 kilometers |

The electromagnetic spectrum covers a vast spread of wavelengths. The only part we can see – the light waves – covers a tiny part of the spectrum. Radio waves take up a huge span from waves about $\frac{4}{100}$ inch (1 mm) long to those of over 60 miles (100 km).

be anything from less than a hundred-million-millionth of a meter for strange cosmic rays that come to us from outer space to thousands of meters for the longest radio waves.

The light waves we can see take up only a very tiny part of the vast spectrum – from 4 to 7 ten-millionths of a meter, as you can see in the diagram above. The waves we can see as the color red are longer than those of the color violet. Other wavelengths in between give us other colors such as yellow and blue.

Different Radio Waves

Radio waves cover a large part of the spectrum. Some of them are great waves miles long, others are tiny wavelets less than $\frac{4}{100}$ inch (1 mm). At the bottom end of the radio wave band are the *microwaves*. These very tiny radio waves are between about 12 inches (30 cm) and less than $\frac{4}{100}$ inch (1 mm) long. Their most important use is in radar, as we have seen. But they are also used to send messages to and from satellites in space. Soon they may be used to beam down the Sun's energy from special power-gathering satellites. Microwaves can also be used for cooking.

Microwaves are made by special tubes called *magnetrons* and *klystrons*. These tubes produce very high frequency waves and amplify then at high powers. Microwaves can also be produced by *solid state* devices. The silicon chip is a solid state device.

Sending Out Microwaves

Microwaves can be modulated, just like ordinary radio waves. They can carry sound waves. These very short waves can be transmitted in narrow beams, while longer radio waves can not. Microwaves need special antennas which are usually shaped like a bowl. And to get the waves from the transmitter to the bowl antenna is not easy. Microwaves get lost if ordinary wires are used. Instead they have to be sent through special "pipes" called *waveguides*.

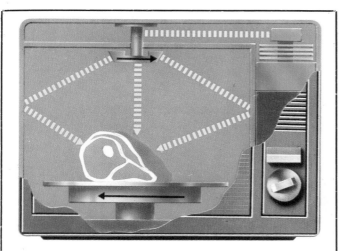

COOKING BY MICROWAVES

Food is cooked in microwave ovens because the waves flip the tiny molecules that make up the food backward and forward, causing heat by friction. The heart of a microwave oven is a valve called a magnetron. This valve makes microwaves that pass along a waveguide and into the oven. These waves oscillate backward and forward over 2000 million times a second and pass through the food being cooked. The rapidly reversing field of the microwaves flips the molecules in the food back and forth. This rapid oscillation of the molecules makes them heat up, so the food is cooked.

The advantage of microwave cooking is that the food is cooked quickly and evenly all the way through. The disadvantage is that there is no browning on the outside, as happens with ordinary ovens.

Shorter and Shorter Waves

As electromagnetic waves get shorter and shorter, they also usually become more penetrating – they pass through things more easily. It is in this very short wavelength part of the spectrum that we meet ultra-violet rays and X-rays.

Just below the part of the electromagnetic spectrum that we can see – the visible light band – lie the ultra-violet rays. These rays have wavelengths less than 16 millionths of an inch, that is, between 4×10^{-7} and 5×10^{-9} meters.

The Sun sends out lots of ultra-violet rays, but, fortunately for us, most of these rays are stopped by the air before they reach us. Very short ultra-violet rays can be quite harmful to our bodies. The rays that do get through are the ones that give us a suntan. We cannot get a suntan through glass because glass stops ultra-violet rays.

The Useful X-rays

Even shorter than ultra-violet rays we come to X-rays. These rays are used a great deal by doctors to see inside us and find out whether there is something wrong. They are also used in industry to inspect materials for internal flaws.

X-rays are absorbed (stopped) at different rates by different materials. Bones, for example, absorb X-rays much more than the softer tissues inside our bodies. When X-rays are passed through us on to a photographic plate, the bones show up as light patches, while the rest of our insides are dark. Anything wrong inside us such as a broken bone, foreign bodies in the lungs or stomach, or arthritis can easily be seen in the photograph.

To find out if there is anything wrong with the stomach or intestines, the patient if given a "barium meal." This consists of drinking a milky liquid made up of barium sulphate. Barium is a metal which stops the X-rays, so the doctor can see exactly what is going on in the patient's stomach as the barium goes down.

Sometimes two X-ray pictures are taken from different angles. This allows the doctor to tell exactly where something such as a bullet is positioned.

Killing Cells with X-rays

X-rays are also used to kill cancers inside the body. This technique can be used by doctors because X-rays damage some kinds of diseased cells more than they do normal cells. But X-rays can also harm us. Too many of these powerful rays can damage healthy tissue. This is why people who operate X-ray apparatus stand behind a lead screen or wear protective clothes.

How X-rays are Generated

X-rays come from a glass tube that has had the air pumped out of it. Electrons are produced at a negative cathode inside the tube by heating it with an electric current. These electrons are pulled towards an anode with a strong positive charge. They strike a "target" made of the metal tungsten set into the anode. When the electrons hit the target, a small part of their energy is turned into X-rays. These rays escape through a small "window" in the well-shielded tube.

Because of the high electrical voltages needed to produce X-rays, the inside of the tube gets very hot. To stop it overheating, the tube has to be water-cooled or the anode has to be made to rotate at speeds of up to 10,000 revolutions per minute.

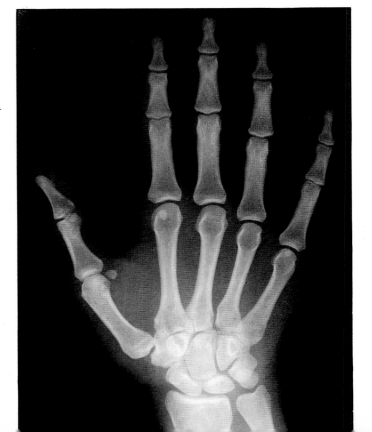

RÖNTGEN'S MYSTERIOUS RAYS

In the year 1895, the German scientist Wilhelm Röntgen was performing some experiments in which he passed high-voltage electric currents through glass tubes that had had most of the air pumped out of them. One day, he noticed that a sheet of photographic paper that had been left near one of the tubes was glowing in the dark. This seemed strange because the glass tube was completely enclosed in cardboard so that no light could escape. Somehow, something coming from the tube was affecting the photographic paper.

Röntgen realized how important his discovery was and he spent the next six weeks without leaving his laboratory, trying to find out all he could about the mysterious rays. He called them "X-rays" because he was not very sure what they were.

Within months of Röntgen's discovery, X-rays were being used to locate some lead pellets that had been accidentally shot into the hand of a New York lawyer.

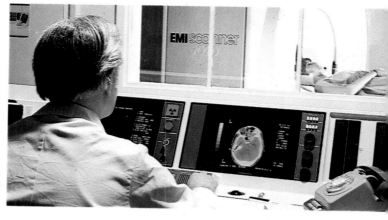

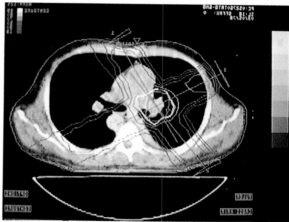

Until recently, X-rays have not been able to show very great detail. This has now changed with the invention of the X-ray scanner, or CAT scanner, shown below right. The scanner is able to take a detailed X-ray picture of a thin slice through the body by X-raying the slice from different angles. A computer then calculates thicknesses within the slice. The result is shown on a screen.

The patient lies on a couch which moves automatically into the scanner until the patient is in the correct position. Then the X-ray machine moves around the patient. The operator controls the scanner from a remote display screen (top).

The center picture shows the scan of a body slice taken across the chest. You can see the spine in the center and the ribs going around it.

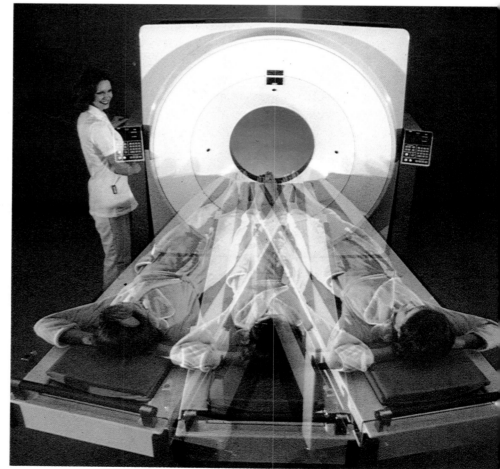

Left: An X-ray picture of a human hand. The waves cloud a photographic plate most when they have passed through flesh, and least when they have passed through bone. Breaks and cracks in the bone will therefore show up clearly on the X-ray.

Before the Computer

THE ABACUS

The first help that people had for counting – apart from their 10 fingers – was the abacus. The abacus was used by the ancient Egyptians and later by the Greeks and Romans because their numbers were very difficult to work with. (How would you like to add CXLVI and XXXVI?)

There are several different kinds of abacus, but they all work in much the same way. The one below is a Chinese abacus. Each column has 2 beads above the crossbar and 5 beads below it. The beads above the crossbar represent 5 units. The lower beads are one unit each.

The right-hand column is the ones column. The second column is the tens, and so on. This means that each bead above the crossbar in the tens column has a value of 50, each bead below the bar in that column has a value of 10. In the hundreds column (the third from the right) the beads below the bar are 100s, those above the bar are 500s.

The number shown in the photograph is 7,230,189. To be counted, a bead must be next to the bar.

When the Arabic system of numbers with the use of the 0 as a number came into being, calculations became much easier and people stopped using the abacus in Europe. However, it is still used in the Orient, the Middle East and in parts of Russia.

Very early in the history of the human race people found out that they could help ease their work by using fire, wheels and levers. Then, as machines became more complicated, people needed new and easier ways of calculating things. They invented the abacus, the calculating machine ... and the computer.

Computers are very new. They only grew up in the second half of the 20th century. Inventions and new developments since about 1945 have made them possible.

But the idea of a computer – of a machine that can do calculations, compare information and store it – goes back at least 150 years. In some ways it goes back much further still, to the invention of the abacus about 5000 years ago in ancient Babylon.

The abacus is the first known calculating machine and it works in a very simple way. (It is still used in parts of the Middle and Far East.) The abacus is only a counting board, with rows of wires or rods onto which blocks or beads are fitted. Each row represents a different category of number (ones, tens, hundreds etc). You add or subtract by moving the beads along the wires. Multiplication is done by repeated addition ($5+5+5+5=5\times4=20$).

Napier's Bones

The next step forward came early in the 17th century. Then the Scottish mathematician John Napier (1550–1617) invented Napier's Bones in the year of his death. The Bones were strips of bone or wood that could be used to multiply and divide, rather like a primitive slide rule. Napier also invented logarithms and the decimal point.

The First Mechanical Calculator

A quarter of a century later came the machine that most people call the first true mechanical calculator. The Pascaline, as it was called, was invented by the French philosopher and mathematician Blaise Pascal in 1642. It consisted of a series of gear wheels with numbers marked on them. The numbers to be added were dialed in, and

Above: Blaise Pascal's calculating machine (1642) was the first true mechanical calculator.
Below: A handloom with jacquard punched cards. Holes in the cards allowed the machine to select threads to make the required pattern. Babbage used the idea of punched cards in his Analytical Engine.

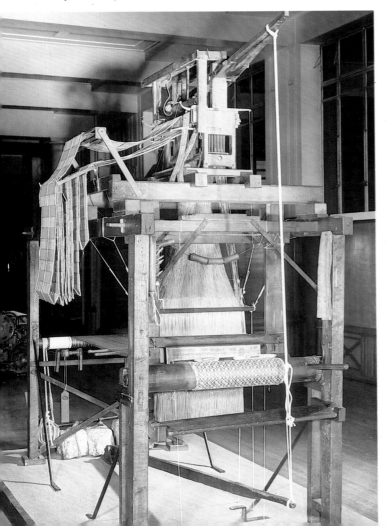

the answer appeared in a window. The gears allowed numbers to be "carried" from tens to hundreds, for instance.

Pascal's machine could only add. The "Stepped Reckoner," invented by the German mathematician Gottfried Leibniz in 1671, could multiply, divide and produce square roots. His machine never worked well in practice. But in theory it was far better than Pascal's.

The First Real Computer

The next great figure is Charles Babbage (1792–1871), a British inventor who spent many years and much money working on, first, a Difference Engine, which was simply a much larger and better version of Pascal's and Leibniz's adding machines. Then he began work on an Analytical Engine. This was developed in 1835 but it never got further than a set of detailed notes called "Observations on Mr. Babbage's Analytical Engine." These notes were written by the Countess of Lovelace, a very good mathematician, who was fascinated by Babbage's work.

Nevertheless, the Analytical Engine was the first real computer. It had some of the same parts as a modern computer, but in a very simple form. It also worked in the same kind of way.

The Analytical Engine had a memory which consisted of groups of 50 counter wheels which could hold 1000 figures of 50 digits each. There

Charles Babbage (above) never actually built his Analytical Engine (left). The machine shown here was made from detailed notes. It was the first real computer.

was an arithmetic unit, known as the mill, which did the calculations. A control unit controlled the order in which the operations were carried out. And there were input and output devices.

The input devices were punched cards. Babbage got the idea for punched cards from those used in cloth weaving to guide the thread into a particular position to make a desired pattern. Plungers went down through holes in the cards to set up a particular sequence of calculations.

Most important of all, the Analytical Engine (which Babbage had planned to be steam-powered) worked in the same way as a modern computer. It could compare numbers and take action depending on the result of the comparison. (This is the IF . . . THEN branch described on page 51.) It could loop, or repeat its program, and could change its program while running.

Sadly, Babbage's ideas stayed on paper and were forgotten, even though a Swedish engineer did build a production model of the Analytical Engine in 1855.

America Takes Over

From Babbage the story leaps half a century and across the Atlantic. It took 7 years to get the results from the 1880 census in the United States. To prevent the same delay with the 1890 census, the US government looked for a new way of

analyzing the census returns. A competition was organized, and the easy winner was a statistician named Herman Hollerith.

Like Babbage's machine, Hollerith's used punched cards. But the similarity ended there. Hollerith's machine was powered by electricity. Each hole in the card represented a different piece of information. Rods passed through the holes and completed an electrical circuit. The counting was done by clocks, which moved on each time a circuit was completed.

Hollerith's invention was a great success and was soon in great demand. Hollerith went into business, and his company later became IBM (International Business Machines) one of the

Hollerith's machine also used punched cards. It was the first electrical calculator.

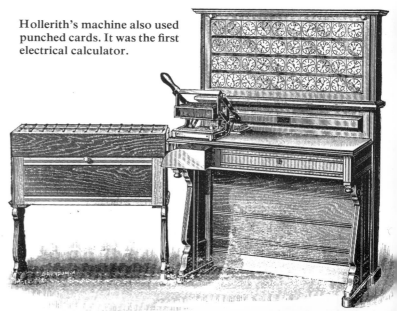

biggest computer companies in the world.

Hollerith's machine was partly electronic, partly mechanical. The next step forward came when an all-electronic machine was developed. This was ENIAC (Electronic Numerical Integrator and Calculator), completed in 1946. In fact, ENIAC was not a real computer but a calculator, since it did not have a memory. But it did work more than 1000 times as fast as the most up-to-date electro-mechanical machines of that time.

A year later came EDVAC (Electronic Discrete Variable Automatic Computer). This was a true computer. It had a memory in which both instructions and data could be stored. And it could change its own programs.

The Thermionic Tube
The secret behind the speed of these early all-electronic computers was the thermionic tube (see page 11). The tubes – ENIAC had no fewer than 18,000 – operated the switching systems that did the calculations.

Tubes worked fast – far faster than any mechanical system could. But they were fragile and bulky, and they only lasted a short time. And because they had to be heated they also used a great deal of electricity.

Tubes marked the beginning of the computer era. But it is transistors that really got it under way.

The Computer Era
Equipped with tubes, computers would have remained bulky, cumbersome machines. Even the earliest transistors, which were invented in 1947, were 100 times smaller than tubes. They were faster and more reliable as well. And they used less electricity, since they did not have to be heated.

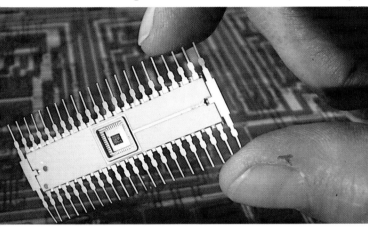

Right: ENIAC, completed in 1946, was the first really electronic machine. It had 18,000 tubes which kept burning out at an alarming rate.
Above right: The Ferranti Mark I was the first commercial computer to appear in Europe, in 1951.
Above: It seems almost impossible that tiny chips like this can do the work of both the machines on the right.

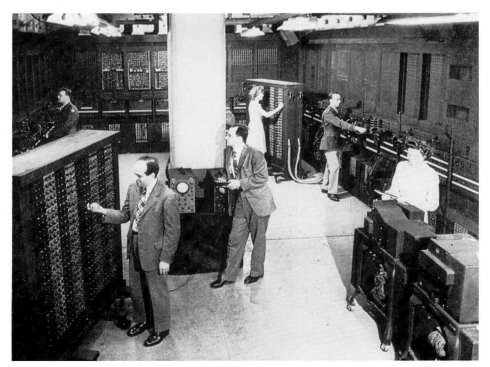

What Can Computers Do?

Every day that passes, the computer is being put to new uses. It is now an essential part of all our lives, whether we realize it or not. Businesses, large and small, are using computers to keep accounts, pay salaries, keep an eye on the stock position. They are used by the police, by banks, by the armed forces, by the airlines and by scientists. This is, without doubt, the age in which the computer grew up.

Computers can only do a few simple tasks. They can add things up. They can subtract things from each other. And they can compare things. But people have to tell computers exactly what to do. Then the computers go ahead and do it.

Why, then, are computers so special? And why is everyone nowadays talking about the "computer revolution"?

Computers work extremely fast; so fast that no person can begin to imagine working at that speed. They can do millions of calculations in a second. This means that the calculations they can do are so complex that no human brain could manage them in a lifetime.

Above: Microcomputers are now becoming an important part of work and play in most schools. More and more young people are coming to realize that the computer is a friend that can help them solve many kinds of problems.

Below: Without the computer, man would never have set foot on the Moon and the Space Shuttle program would have been impossible. This picture shows the Shuttle operations control room during the landing of *Columbia*. The Shuttle can be seen on the large screens.

The three things that computers can do – add, subtract and compare – are usually thought of as arithmetic. When you add 10 to 12, you are doing arithmetic; likewise when you take 7,546,894 from 9,127,985. But although computers work arithmetically, the information they use does not have to start off as numbers. You can use a computer to play games with you or teach you to spell. You can use it to book a seat in an aircraft or a room in a hotel. You can get it to do your accounts for you. You can use it to control robots or alter the direction of a spacecraft in mid-flight or forecast what tomorrow's weather will be.

The information the computer needs to do all these things and many more can start off in many different forms. But before the computer begins to work on it, the information is translated into numbers. (Not into ordinary 0 to 9 numbers but into a special numbering system used by computers. This is explained on pages 44 to 45.)

After the computer has finished its work, the answers have to be translated back again before people can use them.

Making Mistakes

Computers never make mistakes – or only very rarely indeed, when something goes wrong with their circuits.

When computers seem to make a mistake, it is really the people who control them who have done something wrong. Computers do what they are told to do; no more, no less. So long as they are told exactly what to do, in a way they can understand, the right answer will be produced. The wrong answer or a nonsense answer means that someone has given the computer wrong information or wrong instructions.

The point to remember is that computers do not work out *how* to solve a problem. Only people can do that.

Types of Computer

There are three main types of computer – *mainframe, minicomputers,* and *microcomputers.* All of them work in more or less the same way, and most of the descriptions in the following pages apply to them all. The main difference between them is their size – the mainframe is the biggest, the microcomputer the smallest. Their size affects the speed at which they operate and the difficulty of the problems they can tackle. Mainframe computers have a much bigger memory than microcomputers.

Above: Space Shuttle *Columbia's* cabin is a mass of computerized instruments. John Young (left) and Robert Crippen carry out a preflight check.

Below: This carpet design was worked out on a computer.

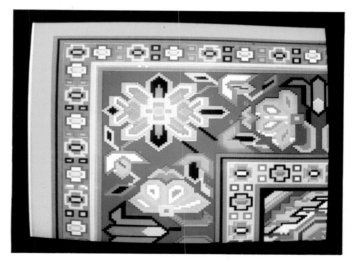

Below: Robots are told exactly what to do by computers. This one is welding two pieces of metal together, with no human being in sight.

How do Computers Work?

A computer is no cleverer than a steam engine. But once it has been told exactly what to do, it will do it in the twinkling of an eye.

So how do computers work? These two pages explain the whole process in outline. The sections that follow, between pages 44 and 57, discuss each aspect in more detail.

At its simplest, a computer has two main parts: a *central processing unit* (CPU) and a *memory*. As its name would lead you to expect, the memory is the place where information is held, or stored. The CPU is the part that does the work. It calculates the answers to the problems with which it is presented.

But on their own these two parts – the memory and the CPU – would be no use at all. Information has to be put into the computer so that the memory has something to hold and the CPU something to process. And other information – the results of the computer's work – has to be taken out so that we can use it. The pieces of equipment that do this work are called the *input* and *output*

devices or *peripherals*. The most common input device is a keyboard rather like a typewriter keyboard. The most common output device is a television screen, linked to the computer.

Other kinds of equipment can be used as input and output devices. Many of these will be mentioned later in the book. The variety of input and output peripherals is extremely important. It gives computers their versatility and allows them to be used in all kinds of activities.

All the equipment mentioned so far is known in computer jargon as "hardware."

The Electronics of Computing

The silicon chip (see page 14) lies right at the heart of modern computing. The whole CPU of a small computer can be fitted onto one chip. The memory needs more – 32 chips in a typical microcomputer. The chip itself, as we have seen, acts as an

The most popular way of getting information into a computer is through a keyboard like this. It looks much like a typewriter keyboard, but this one has a separate group of keys for numbers – just like a calculator. Pressing a key sends a series of electronic pulses into the computer.

integrated circuit, consisting of thousands of tiny transistors and other devices.

The computer is powered by electricity. Electronic signals sent out at fantastically high speeds work the central processing unit and put information into the memory and take it out again. The information itself is carried by patterns of electric current in binary form. So are the instructions to the computer telling it what to do with the information.

An electric current can either be on or off; one thing or the other. So all the information being stored in or used by the computer has to be coded as one of two numbers – 0 or 1. This numbering system is called the binary system (see page 44). The numbering system we use every day has ten numbers, 0 to 9. Put simply, each electronic circuit in a computer repesents a 1 when it is conducting and a 0 when it is not.

Communicating With the Computer

Computers only understand binary numbers. To a computer, the figure 2 is 0010, 4 is 0100. All the numbers that we can write using the ten figures 0 to 9 can be represented in the binary system by 0s and 1s. It is just a matter of translating them.

To instruct a computer to do something you have to write a program. Writing a program in binary numbers – nothing but 0s and 1s – would be time-consuming and tiring. Computers would not be so cheap and simple to use if we had to think in binary numbers. So a neat and simple solution has been found. The computer itself has been programmed to translate its instructions into the binary system – into *machine language*, as it is known. Every computer has one of these programs built in, which automatically translates our instructions into machine language.

Normally computer programmers – whether professionals at work or people who have a microcomputer at home – use what are known as "high level" languages. These are quite like everyday English and are quite easy to learn. Four of the most common are BASIC, which was first designed for beginners, FORTRAN, for mathematics, COBOL, for business, and the newer LOGO designed for children. You write the program in, say, BASIC. The computer translates it into machine language (binary) and then – and only then – carries out the instructions on the program.

There is one final snag. Programming a

This is a blown-up picture of a computer's memory chip. The chip is the rectangle in the center and it is connected to the outside world by about 40 gold wires much finer than hairs. This chip can hold 16,384 bits of information.

computer is not simply a matter of telling it to check whether there are two seats free on the night flight to New York. The program has to tell the computer exactly what to do at every point and in the right order. If any step is omitted, or if anything is not exactly clear and straightforward, the program will not work.

Computers can be made to do almost anything. The boy below is playing with a computer "turtle" that draws geometrical shapes and patterns. It is designed to help handicapped children draw and recognize forms that would otherwise be difficult for them. The turtle is worked by a microcomputer and can be controlled by a special touch sensitive keyboard. These keyboards can be worked by children who could not write instructions on an ordinary keyboard. The computer can be programmed to understand that when a certain part of the board is touched, then it should draw a cow, say, or perform some other instruction.

Counting in 0s and 1s

Computers can only count up to 1! They can be programmed to recognize a flow of current or no flow of current – 1 or 0. So the two numerals 1 and 0 are very important to computers. This is why people who make computers have to find a way of turning our decimal numbers into 1s and 0s before asking the computer to work on them. They use the binary system.

A bit is a binary digit. The picture shows how we get the word. The information or instructions we put into a computer has to be turned into binary information. When we type information or instructions into a computer, there are special chips in the machine that change our English words or numbers into binary code. The binary code that the computer uses is called *machine code*.

Counting in 0s and 1s – in binary numbers – might seem difficult at first. But the principle is the same as in the decimal system we use in everyday life.

Our decimal system works in tens, maybe because we have ten fingers and have been using them to count with for thousands of years. In a three-figure number, the left-hand figure stands for hundreds, the middle figure for tens and the right-hand figure for units. So the number 137 represents one hundred, three tens and seven units.

The binary system works in exactly the same way. The only difference is that the columns are based on twos, not on tens. So, reading from right to left, the first column of a binary number stands for units; the second, twos; the third, fours; the fourth, eights; the fifth, sixteens; the sixth, thirty-twos, and so on. So, in binary numbers, 137 is written 10001001 – 1 one, no twos, no fours, 1 eight, no sixteens, no thirty-twos, no sixty-fours, and 1 one hundred and twenty-eight.

Binary numbers are also used in computers to represent the letters of the alphabet and punctuation marks – ; . , and so on – and also the space between words. An international agreement lays down the agreed code for each letter and piece of punctuation. For instance, capital T is 01010100 and ? is 00111111.

Bits and Bytes

The smallest unit of information in a computer is called a *bit*. The word is short for BInary digiT. A bit is a single binary number – in other words, a single electrical pulse. A *byte* consists of a group of 8 bits. This is the basic computing unit in most microcomputers. Each location in a microcomputer's memory can hold a single byte.

Both *data* – the information the computer is given to work on – and the program (the instructions that tell it what to do with the data) are in the form of bytes. The way in which the bytes are coded allows the computer to tell the difference.

THE BINARY TABLE

Binary numbers seem rather awkward to us – almost like going back to unwieldy Roman numerals. But the binary system is the only one computers recognize, and because the computer operates at such a fantastic speed it can churn its way through millions of 0s or 1s before we can add 2 and 2.

Decimal	Binary
1	0001
2	0010
3	0011
4	0100
5	0101
6	0110
7	0111
8	1000

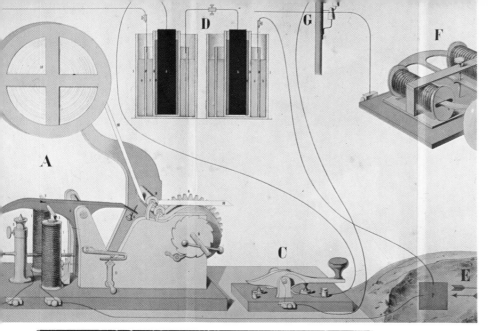

The Morse Code, invented by Samuel Morse in 1837, is rather like a binary system. It depends on one important fact: whether an electric current is flowing or whether it is not. The old diagram on the left shows how Morse's system was used to send signals along telegraph wires.

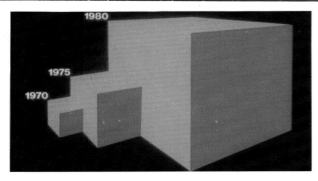

HOW THE BITS HAVE GROWN

The block graph above gives some idea of how quickly the silicon chip has advanced. In 1970, scientists were able to squeeze little more than a hundred binary digits or bits of information onto a single chip. By 1980, the density had increased much more than a hundredfold – 70,000 bits on a chip were quite common. Scientists are now talking about a million bits on a chip – and the price is falling at the same time.

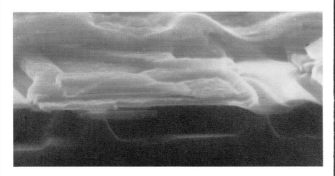

DEEP INSIDE A CHIP

The picture above gives a view of a silicon chip that can only be achieved by using a powerful electron microscope. It is magnified well over 5000 times and shows only a tiny part of the little chip. You can see the different layers of the integrated circuit. It is these very small circuits that handle the 1s and 0s of binary – electrical current or no electrical current. The picture on the right shows the size of the whole chip. The "rope" is sewing cotton in the eye of the needle.

The Computer's Heart and Memory

No one has yet built a computer with a memory as great as that of the human brain. But once it is told something, a computer will never forget it.

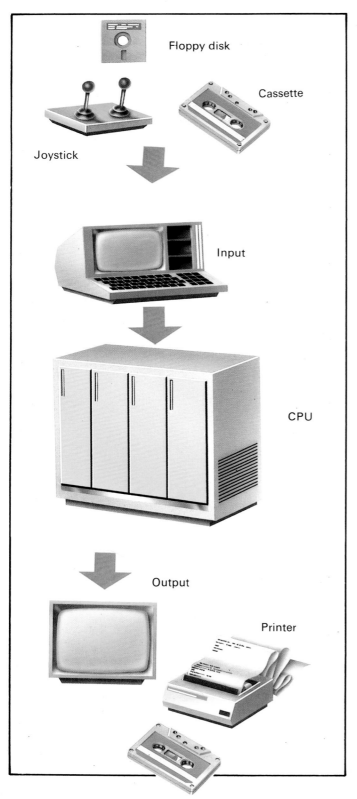

Floppy disk

Cassette

Joystick

Input

CPU

Output

Printer

The heart of the computer is the *central processing unit* (CPU for short). It is the link between the input and output devices and the memory, and it keeps them all working in the right order. All the information with which the computer works has to travel through the CPU. But the CPU is much more than a glorified information traffic junction. It is also the place where the computer does its computing; where the arithmetic operations – adding, subtracting and comparing – actually take place.

The Memory

A computer's memory is its store of information. It is the place where the computer keeps all the information that has been fed into it.

But a memory doesn't just consist of a great pile of electrical impulses. It is carefully organized so that the information is easy to get at. It is rather like a dictionary, which is another type of information store. In a dictionary, the words do not lie about in a disorganized mess. Every word in the dictionary has its own address, which helps you to find it. So to look up the word "computer" you first look among the words starting with "c," then among those starting with "co," then "com" and so on. You don't look for it among the words starting with "s," since that is the wrong address.

The dictionary information store is organized in alphabetical order. The computer's is arranged in memory locations, or boxes. Each of these usually contains one byte (8 bits) of information. Information that takes up more than 8 digits has to be stored in more than one box. So the biggest number that can fit into one memory box is 255, which in binary numbers is written 11111111.

The big difference between a dictionary and a computer memory is that it makes no difference where in the computer's memory the information is stored. In a dictionary, all the words starting with "c" are stored under "c." If you put words just anywhere – "computer" between "kangaroo" and "windmill," for instance – it would be almost

Left: The central processing unit (CPU) is the heart of the computer. It does all the adding, subtracting and comparing. Into it we feed information by means of keyboards, tapes, disks or the joysticks we use in video games. The output from the CPU can go to many things, including TV screens, printers and tapes.

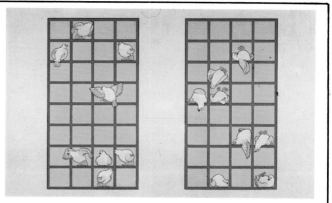

THE COMPUTER'S MEMORIES

The picture on the left shows 32 pigeon holes, arranged in 8 rows of 4. Let us say that a pigeon in a hole is binary 1 and an empty hole is binary 0. So each row of holes can represent up to 15 (15 = binary 1111). Each hole holds 1 bit of information, so the whole memory can store 32 bits of information.

Memories in computers are arranged in rows like this – rows of 4 as here, or, more often, rows of 8 or 16. Here, each row of 4 holes is called a 4-bit word.

Suppose we want to store the number 10 in our memory. In binary, 10 is 1010 (no 1s, one 2, no 4s, and one 8). Now look at row 3 in the memory. It is enlarged in the circle. The row number is called the *address* of that row. We have stored the number 10 in address 3. In binary numbers, we have stored 1010 in address 0011.

Computers have two basic kinds of electronic memory. In the third picture, all the pigeons are alive – they can fly in and out of the holes as they wish. This represents changing information in the memory. We call this memory the RAM (Random Access Memory). We can write into it as well as read from it.

In the fourth picture, all the pigeons are dead. They represent information that, once it is put into a hole, is there for good and can't be changed. This kind of memory is called ROM (Read Only Memory). We can read this information, but we can't write information into the ROM.

impossible to find any of them. Not so in the computer. It matters not at all where in the memory information is stored. The computer can find any piece of information in a quarter of a millionth of a second. All you have to do is give the computer the address of the memory location and the machine will find it.

Different Kinds of Memory

There are two main types of computer memory, known as RAM and ROM. RAM stands for Random Access Memory. ROM stands for Read Only Memory.

RAM is the computer's working memory. You can put information into it – or *write* it in – and you can take information out of it – or *read* it. This is why a RAM is sometimes called a read/write memory.

When you write information into a RAM memory location, the information it held before is wiped out. But when you read the information that location holds, it is merely copied. The information itself remains in its memory location.

RAMs are short-term memories only. As soon as you switch off the computer, the entire contents of the RAM are lost forever unless you record these contents on a tape or a disk.

ROMs are Different

ROMs are quite different. They are built-in memories that can only be read. You cannot write any new information into them, nor can you wipe their information out. Most ROMs contain programs that help the computer do its job. For instance, ROM holds the program that translates your BASIC instructions into machine language that the computer can understand. The computer operator has no control over it. ROMs also hold the CPU's operating instructions which tell it how to get hold of information in the RAM.

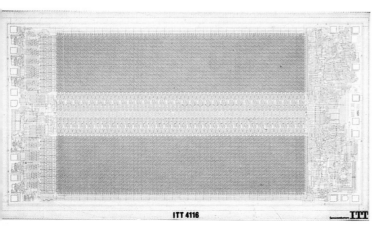

ITT 4116   ITT

The picture on the left was taken through a microscope. It shows a memory chip. You can see how complicated it is.

Helping the Computer's Memory

If a computer only had a RAM and a ROM, it would not be particularly useful. Every time you used the computer you would have to type in a great deal of information – information which you may have typed in the day before and wiped out when you switched the computer off. This would be a great waste of time.

In fact, much of a computer's memory lies outside the main machine itself. This back-up memory is contained on magnetic disks or on cassette tapes. The general name for these extra memories is *software*. Software can consist of almost anything. A program might be for a Star Wars game, or for a game of chess, or to check spelling, to prepare monthly pay checks – or 101 other things. The information these programs hold can be fed into a computer's RAM in a very short time.

Back-up memories, or stores, are not like RAMs. Unlike the contents of a RAM, you cannot wipe them out, unless you deliberately choose to. They exist even when the machine is switched off. They are really extensions to the machine's RAM that can be used again and again.

What the Memory Contains

Up to now, the contents of a computer's memory have been described as "information." But in fact this kind of information takes two different forms: *data* and *instructions*. Data means pieces of

Above: One chip cannot hold all the information we need in a computer. There are lots of chips, and each one can be controlled separately.

information. If I tell the computer my first name is John, my second name Charles and my third Smith, those are three pieces of data that the machine will store in its memory. But if I tell the computer to print my names, I give it an

Below: Different kinds of extra memory for the computer. Information can be stored on tape (bottom), on large or small floppy disks (right) or on large hard disks (top).

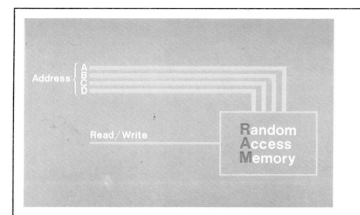

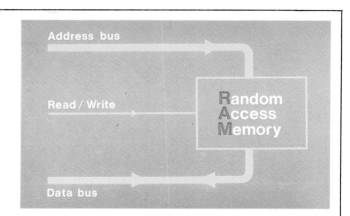

HOW A RAM WORKS

The picture on the left shows very simply a RAM in use. First of all, the memory needs to know which memory line you want to look at or write on. Think about the 8 lines of 4-bit words on the previous page. Our memory has a 4-bit address, so we need 4 wires going to the chip. They go to addresses.

Suppose we feed in the code for memory line 5 – binary 0101 – on the wires A, B, C, and D. Now there is a fifth wire, labelled Read/Write. If we hold the electrical voltage high on that wire, the chip knows we want to *read* the information on the line given by the binary code on the address wires 0101. If we hold the voltage low on the Read/Write wire, the chip will allow us to write in

information on that same line.

In the picture on the right, instead of the 4 address wires we have drawn one wire. This wire we call an *address bus*. In a 4-bit system, the bus would be 4 wires, in an 8-bit system it would be 8 wires.

But now there is another bundle of wires at the bottom. This bundle shows how information gets into the memory and how it can be got out. As this bundle of wires carries the information that we want, it is called a *data bus*. If we put an address on the address bus and tell the memory to *read*, the information on that memory line is switched to the data bus.

If we instruct the chip to *write*, whatever is put on the data bus is written into the location which we've put on the address bus. So information goes both ways on the data bus – but only in one direction at a time.

---

instruction. Pages 51 to 55, which explain programming, show how the computer is told the difference between data and instructions. But both kinds of information are present in the same program. You do not have to write one program to contain data and another for instructions.

Inside the Computer

What happens inside a computer? We have talked about data and instructions being sent from an input device to the memory via the CPU. Then it goes back again to the CPU and on to some kind of output device. But how does this happen?

Taking the Bus

There are "buses" inside every computer. A bus is a set of wires running from the CPU to the memory. Think of them as a set of footpaths along which information, coded in electrical pulses, travels. Although each bus has the same starting point and the same destination, they each take a different route to get there.

The buses are the *address bus*, the *control bus* and the *data bus*. The address bus is for the address of the memory box. The control bus says what will happen at the memory box: information will either

be entered or copied. And the data bus carries the information itself – either instructions or data.

The name John Smith is to be written into the memory. The address bus carries the address of the memory box where the name is to go. The control bus carries the order to write the name in. And the data bus carries the data – in this case the name John Smith.

Pulses and Switches

The CPU and the two memories – RAM and ROM – are made up of hundreds of circuits, each containing lots of tiny transistor switches. These are the key to the binary system. A switch can either be on or off. If it is on, the circuit is conducting. If it is off, the circuit is not conducting. The binary digit 0 signifies "off." The digit 1 signifies "on." It takes just a few thousandths of a millionth of a second to turn a switch on or off.

A clock inside the computer produces a huge number of electrical pulses – several million a second. These pulses are sent running on special paths through the computer. Their paths are determined by the make-up of each byte – its combination of 0s and 1s.

Analogue and Digital

The computers we have been looking at can only work with *digital* information. Binary numbers, with which computers work, are one kind of digital system. Decimal numbers (0 to 9) are another.

But often the information the computer uses comes in *analogue* (constantly varying) form. A computer might have the job of controlling the temperature of a greenhouse, making sure that it is always exactly right for the plants. Data, in this case the temperature in the greenhouse, will come from temperature sensors. But the temperature varies constantly.

The difference between digital and analogue is best explained by looking at two watches – one ordinary watch with hour and minute hands, the other digital that jumps from second to second. The digital watch shows time in the form of numbers. It is programmed to change, say, every second. The minute hand of the ordinary watch moves round the dial steadily, without pausing.

The problem for computers is to turn analogue information, which they cannot handle, into digital information, which they can. This is done by an analogue converter. The converter measures the analogue data – time, temperature, water flow, pressure or whatever – at regular and frequent intervals. It inputs this information into the computer. So long as the computer also knows how frequently the measurements have been

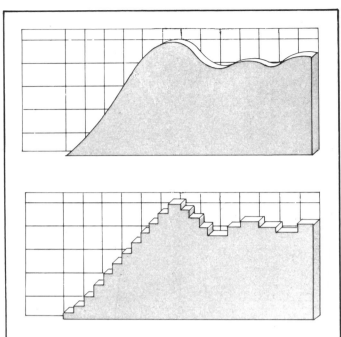

There were two quite different kinds of computer in the early days – analogue computers and digital computers.

Analogue computers work by following exactly whatever they are computing. As a pointer on a dial moves to different positions, the computer follows that movement continuously. If a voltage changes, the analogue computer changes with it. This is shown by the top curve.

Digital computers turn everything into numbers, whether they are dealing with voltages, words or anything else. Information passes through them in jumps or pulses. The bottom curve shows very roughly how the top curve would appear in a digital computer. The smaller the steps, the closer the digital curve will come to be like the analogue curve.

taken, it can produce a digital version of what is happening.

The ability to turn analogue to digital measurements is very important. It allows computers to be put to work in many different types of industry.

Until quite recently, all our time-keeping devices were analogue – they showed the passing of time in continuous movement. Digital clocks and watches progress in jumps.

A DIGITAL WATCH

The picture on the left below shows the inside of an ordinary digital watch. Like most watches of this kind, it has a quartz crystal (shown by the pink arrow) that vibrates at 32,768 hertz (32,768 times per second). It vibrates at this very fast rate because the crystal has to be small to fit into the watch. And the smaller the crystal the faster it vibrates.

The crystal is made to vibrate by a tiny electronic circuit – an oscillator. The blue arrow shows the capacitor in that circuit. The crystal controls the rate of vibration very accurately. A tiny silicon chip cuts down the vibration rate to a speed that can be used to let us tell the time.

Writing Programs

Before we can get a computer to do anything, someone has to give it information. And we also have to tell the machine exactly how to handle this information. This is done by writing a program which the computer can follow, step by step in a very laborious way.

What is your program every morning when you arrive at school? It could be:

1 Walk around the playground.
2 Go inside.
3 Walk upstairs.
4 Sit down at your place.

You do that every morning without even thinking about it. You don't arrive outside school and think: What happens next? You just carry out the program automatically.

But what if you didn't know the routine? How would you tell someone exactly what to do? Look at the first instruction on the morning program. It takes it for granted that you have walked into the playground. But if you were describing everything in detail, you would have to start: Walk into playground.

Look too at the third and fourth instructions. There's a lot that's missing between them. If a stranger had to find your place, you would have to add these instructions:

4   Turn left at the top of the stairs.
5   Walk along corridor.
6   Find fifth door on the right.
7   Enter door.
8   Walk down nearest side of room.
9   Find third row of chairs.
10 Walk along row.
11 Find fourth chair.
12 Sit on it.

This program is quite sufficient for anyone to follow without difficulty. But, if you think about it, you will realize that it ignores all kinds of possibilities. It doesn't allow you to spend longer in the playground if you have arrived early. It doesn't allow you to stop and talk to friends, or to avoid someone you don't like.

In other words, it ignores all the decisions you make on the spur of the moment. *If* you see your friend Alison, *then* you stop to talk to her. If you see her, you change the original program. You go along a branch and then return to the original program later.

There are a lot of other if . . . then decisions the program ignores. *If* you see someone coming toward you, *then* you move out of the way. *If* someone trips over, *then* you stop to help them up. And so on.

Imagine you had a computerized robot. Think of all the possibilities you would have to allow for in writing a program to get it safely into your seat at school.

MAKING A COMPUTER WORK

Let us suppose that you sit down at the computer and switch it on. Now type on the keyboard PRINT 4 + 2 and press the key marked RETURN or, in some computers NEW LINE or ENTER. The computer answers at once by showing the figure 6.

The word PRINT tells the computer to show us whatever we have asked for – in this case the answer to 4 + 2.

But if you type PRINT "4 + 2" and press the RETURN key, the computer again does exactly as you tell it. It prints 4 + 2, like this:

4 + 2

This shows what a big difference the quotation marks make. Anything we type in between quotation marks will appear exactly as it is – but without the quotation marks. Anything between quotation marks – figures, letters or punctuation marks – is called a *string*. The computer regards a string as just a meaningless jumble of symbols. It doesn't try to do anything with them. It just remembers them.

Can you think what the computer will produce if you type this:

PRINT "4 + 2 = "; 4 + 2

On the screen appears

4 + 2 = 6

The 4 + 2 between the quotation marks appears as you typed it. The other 4 + 2, the computer adds to make 6. You had to put the = sign between the quotation marks because you wanted the computer to print that.

The semicolon is an important sign in computers. If it is *outside* quotation marks, it tells the computer to print the next thing on the screen right up against the first. If we used a comma instead of a semicolon, the 6 would be a good distance from the 4 + 2, like this:

4 + 2 =   6

The comma tells the computer to move along the screen a bit.

You can't leave anything out when you are programming. A computer assumes nothing. It simply works on the information it is given. Imagine, then, writing a program for stair-climbing. It would be no use saying "Walk up the stairs," as you can to a real person. The program would have to be something like:

1 Lift right leg.
2 Place it on step.
3 Lift left leg.
4 Place it on step.

That is fine as far as it goes – which is not very far. All it does is get the robot from one step to the next. But there is nothing to say how many steps there are to climb and when the robot has reached the top.

Let us assume that there are 18 steps. You could write out the program above another 17 times. But that would be clumsy and long-winded. Instead, you can put a *loop* in the program. A loop is

exactly what it says it is: a part of the program that goes round and round. When you get to the end of the loop, you start at the beginning again, and so on.

The only problem with a loop is how to get out of it. If you put a stair-climbing loop in the program, the robot will go on trying to climb stairs forever, since it has not been told how many there are.

How, then, do you program the robot to climb 18, and not 17 or 19 steps? The solution is to put in a *variable*. (We will learn more about variables later.) In this case we would put a line into the program saying: LET steps = 0. This may sound rather silly at first, but remember we are dealing with a computer, and computers can be silly. Anyway, this part of our program would read:

1 LET steps = 0
2 Lift right leg
3 Place it on next step up
4 Lift left leg

Continued on page 54.

Unless we program the robot to stop climbing at a certain step, it will go on trying to climb forever...

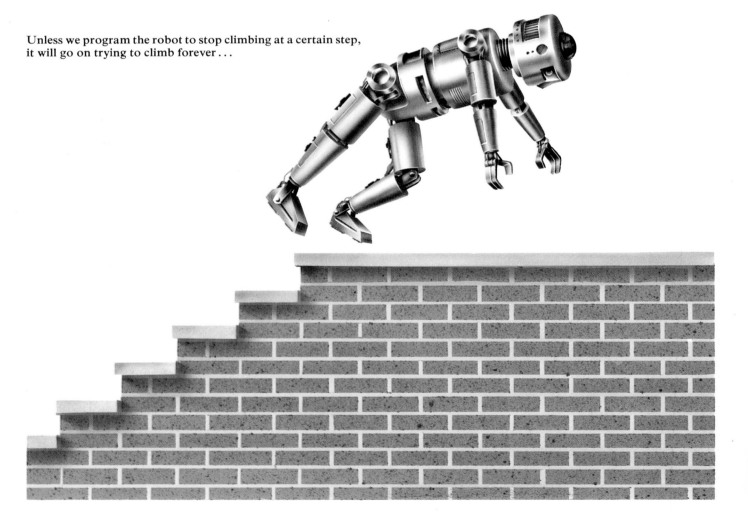

LOOPS

Building loops into a program is quite simple. A loop may often result in a short program that can do a large amount of work. Here is a simple program with a loop.

```
10 PRINT "COST OF ITEM"
20 INPUT C
30 IF C <0 THEN GOTO 60
40 LET RT=RT+C
50 GOTO 10
60 PRINT "TOTAL COST="; RT
70 END
```

This program simply adds up a list of costs, which can be as long or short as you like. In line 20, C stands for the cost of each item. In line 40, RT stands for the running total. You can see how the loop works when you type in RUN. The computer screen reads:

```
COST OF ITEM
?
```

We type in the cost of the first item – say 24 – and the screen looks lke this:

```
COST OF ITEM
?24
COST OF ITEM
?
```

We type in the cost of the second item – say 20 – and the screen looks like this:

```
COST OF ITEM
?24
COST OF ITEM
?20
```

Each time we type in a cost, the computer asks us for another one. This would go on for ever if we didn't have some way of ending the loop. Each time we type in a cost, the computer goes on from line 20 to line 30. This line tells it that if the cost is less than 0 it has to go to line 60. But the cost is never less than 0, so it goes to line 40. Line 40 tells the computer to add the last cost to the running total. It does this and stores the result in its memory. Then it goes to line 50. Line 50 tells it to go back to line 10, so the computer prints COST OF ITEM again and waits for another cost to be entered. So long as you go on adding costs each time line 20 is reached, the loop will run and run – literally forever. But what happens when you have typed in all your costs? How do you get the computer to produce a final total?

This is where line 30 comes in. To break the circle you simply type in any imaginary cost – as long as it is less than 0. A cost of −1 or −28 or any other minus quantity will do. Line 30 tells the computer that if it receives a minus cost it is to go to line 60. (Remember that the < sign means "less than.") So the computer prints the total cost, which is the running total.

Flowcharts are often used to show how a program works. One for this program would look like the one on the left.

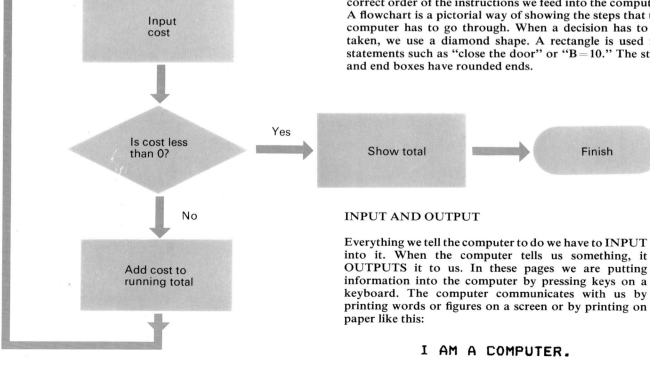

Flowcharts like the one on the left help us to understand the correct order of the instructions we feed into the computer. A flowchart is a pictorial way of showing the steps that the computer has to go through. When a decision has to be taken, we use a diamond shape. A rectangle is used for statements such as "close the door" or "B=10." The start and end boxes have rounded ends.

INPUT AND OUTPUT

Everything we tell the computer to do we have to INPUT into it. When the computer tells us something, it OUTPUTS it to us. In these pages we are putting information into the computer by pressing keys on a keyboard. The computer communicates with us by printing words or figures on a screen or by printing on paper like this:

I AM A COMPUTER.

5 Place it on step
6 LET steps = steps + 1
7 IF steps <18 THEN GO TO 2
8 Turn left
and so on.

The sign < means "less than." The variable appears at line 1 and again at line 6. At line 6 it equals 1 (0+1), because 1 step has been climbed. Line 7 is the loop. If the variable in line 6 is less than 18, the loop sends the computer back to line 2. This goes on happening until the top of the stairs is reached. Then steps are no longer less than 18 but the same, and the computer goes to line 8.

Finding your classroom place is not a real computer program. But it does show that you have to tell the computer exactly what to do. You must think of everything in small easy stages. If you don't, the program won't work. Everything must be planned in exactly the right order. The computer can be programmed to take decisions (if ... then), and it can continue to do the same operation over and over again.

Tackling a Real Program

This is a very simple example of a real program. It has been written in BASIC and it will work on most microcomputers. If you don't have your own computer, it will give you some idea of what happens. If you do have one, you can try it yourself – and improve on it.

We want to program the computer to add the cost of goods bought on a shopping trip. The program will run like this:

```
10 PRINT "ADDING UP THE COST"
20 PRINT "COST OF APPLES"
30 INPUT A
40 PRINT "COST OF BREAD"
50 INPUT B
60 PRINT "COST OF CHEESE"
70 INPUT C
80 LET D = A + B + C
90 PRINT "TOTAL COST = "; D
100 END
```

Lines 10, 20, 40, 60 and 90 begin with the word PRINT. When we type this word into the computer it will display on the screen whatever we type between the quotation marks after the word PRINT. If we type PRINT "JOHN SMITH", the computer will faithfully display JOHN SMITH on the screen.

Lines 30, 50, and 70 begin with the word INPUT. This lets us put information into the program while the program is running. You will

---

A FIRST PROGRAM

Here is a very simple program to start with:

```
10 PRINT "WHAT IS YOUR NAME?"
20 INPUT A$
30 PRINT "HELLO, "; A$
40 END
```

Line 10 tells the computer to print on the screen WHAT IS YOUR NAME? – everything between the quotation marks.

Line 20 tells the computer to set aside a memory box labelled A$ and wait for something to put in the box.

Line 30 tells the computer to print HELLO, followed immediately by whatever is in the A$ memory box.

So, if we type RUN, this appears on the screen:

```
RUN
WHAT IS YOUR NAME?
?
```

The computer waits until you type in something to fill the A$ box. Let's suppose you type CAROLINE. The computer immediately says, HELLO, CAROLINE.

Notice the space after HELLO, the semicolon tells the computer to print CAROLINE immediately after HELLO, so it is better to leave a space after HELLO.

You will have noticed the dollar sign $ at the end of INPUT A$. The dollar sign lets the computer know that letters, not numbers, are going to be put into this memory box.

There are two kinds of variable – two kinds of memory box. The first kind is a *numeric variable*. This can only have numbers in it. You can use letters of the alphabet or words as labels for this kind of memory box (INPUT A or INPUT AC or INPUT A2 or INPUT AGE).

The second kind of memory box is called a *string variable*. A string variable can be anything we choose, words, letters, numbers, punctuation marks or a mixture of all of them. The labels for all string variables must end with the dollar sign $.

For example, we can have a little program like this:

```
10 LET C$ = "HUNGRY MICE"
20 LET A = 8
30 LET B$ = "ATE"
40 LET A$ = "HUNGRY CATS"
50 LET C = 8
60 PRINT A
70 PRINT A$
80 PRINT B$
90 PRINT C
100 PRINT C$
110 END
```

END tells the computer it is the end of the program. Some computers must have this statement, others don't need it. Can you work out what will appear on the screen?

notice that at the end of each of these lines there is a letter, A, B etc. These are the labels by which the computer remembers the information we put into the line. If the program has a line, 30 INPUT A, when the program is RUN, the computer stops at line 30 and asks us to put in some information. When we type in the information – the data – the computer stores it in memory box A. A labelled memory box is called a *variable* because it can hold different bits of information at different times during the program. When you put data into a memory box, it wipes out any data that was there before. So if you put 10 into a variable and then 9, it will hold the figure 9, not 10 or 19.

Running the Program

When we have finished typing in our program we type RUN. This makes the computer start carrying out our instructions. On the screen appears:

RUN
ADDING UP THE COST
COST OF APPLES
?

The question mark tells us that the computer wants some information – in this case the cost of the apples.

We type in 1.10 (meaning $1.10), and the screen reads:

RUN
ADDING UP THE COST
COST OF APPLES
? 1.10
COST OF BREAD
?

We type in what we spent on bread, and the screen shows:

RUN
ADDING UP THE COST
COST OF APPLES
? 1.10
COST OF BREAD
? .45
COST OF CHEESE
?

The cost of cheese was 68¢, so we type in .68, and

the screen shows:

RUN
ADDING UP THE COST
COST OF APPLES
? 1.10
COST OF BREAD
? .45
COST OF CHEESE
? .68
TOTAL COST = 2.23

As soon as we type in the 68¢ for cheese the computer shows the total cost.

Can you work out how the computer managed to do this? At line 80 we told it to add A, B and C and store in box D. Line 90 tells the computer to print everything between the quotation marks, followed by D, which is the total cost.

This may seem a lot of effort to solve a very simple addition sum. It is; we wouldn't use a computer for a sum like this. But in working out the program we have found out quite a lot about how a computer works.

Some computers vary a bit. Some, for example, have some other symbol instead of a question mark when the computer wants you to give it some information. But all computers have a figure 0 like this to show that it is a zero and not the letter O.

You will have noticed that we have numbered the lines of our program in tens from 10 to 100. Unless it is told otherwise, the computer starts at the lowest line number and works its way to the end of the program. You will find, however, that most programs contain instructions to make the computer jump back and forth inside the program.

The line numbers tell the computer to store the instructions in its memory and hold them there until they are needed. Only when we type RUN does the computer start work on the program.

Line numbers in BASIC usually jump in 10s. The reason for this is quite simple. Should we want to add a new line or lines into our program we can do so. We can add new lines 15 and 16 between 10 and 20 and the computer will sort it out.

One other thing: Every microcomputer keyboard has a key labelled RETURN or ENTER or NEWLINE. This key has to be pressed at the end of each line of the program. If this key isn't pressed the computer continues on the same line until it gets to the end, when it returns to the beginning of the next line.

Talking to the Computer

On their own, the CPU and memory are useless. They cannot do anything unless they are given data to work on and instruction about what to do with it. This is known as *input*.

The CPU and memory also have to be able to do something with the results. They have to put it out in one form or another. This is called *output*.

The equipment that makes this possible is known by a variety of names: input and output devices, peripheral devices, or simply *peripherals*. The word "peripheral" is a good one. It suggests that these devices are on the periphery, or edge, of

People usually communicate with computers through keyboards. Keyboards vary quite a lot, but they all have the letters of the alphabet in the same order. The keyboard below is a specialized one. It has a separate group of number keys.

the computer. In other words, they connect the computer's internal systems with the outside world.

The input device on most microcomputers is a keyboard. This is rather like the keyboard on a conventional typewriter. The letters and numbers are arranged in the same order, and there are keys for punctuation marks and symbols such as & and %. In addition, there are keys for special computer commands. These keys can be different from one make of computer to another.

When you strike a key, electronic signals are passed to the computer, where they are translated into machine language that the computer understands.

It's on the Screen

Keyboards are usually linked to a *visual display unit* (VDU), often an ordinary television screen. The information typed into the computer also appears on the screen. For some users of home computers this is enough. They have to put up with the disadvantage that whatever is on the screen vanishes forever as soon as they switch the power off.

A printer gives a more permanent record. As you type the information into the computer, the printer prints it on a sheet of paper.

The cheapest form of printer is the *teletypewriter*. It is slow (only about 10 characters a second) and it only prints in capitals.

Dot matrix printers are the most common type. They work by firing groups of needles at the paper – each group produces a different character. If you look closely at a printed dot matrix character you will see that it is made up of tiny dots. Dot matrix printing is quite suitable for most purposes.

Daisy-wheel printers are more expensive. The wheel has up to 100 characters, each character being on its own arm of the wheel. The characters are struck by a tiny hammer. This type of printer gives the best final result.

Floppy Disks and Cassettes

Floppy disks and *cassettes* are another form of input/output. To use them you need a *disk drive* or an ordinary cassette tape recorder. You simply link the drive or tape recorder to the computer by plugging them in and switching on. The program on the disk or cassette goes into the computer's RAM memory or is taken out of the RAM onto the disk or cassette.

It takes much less time to find a piece of information or an entire program on a disk than on a cassette. The cassette tape has to run all the way through until it reaches the part you are looking for. This is called *sequential access*. The disk can jump to the right part in a few seconds. This is called *random access*.

Other Input/Outputs

Keyboards, VDUs, printers, tape cassettes and disk drives are the main peripherals used with home computers.

One computer can also act as the peripheral of a second computer. This is a most important feature. It makes networks of computers possible, with information being passed in just a few seconds over long distances, perhaps across the world. The link is usually by telephone. Each computer does its own work but can also transfer information to any of the others in the network.

Telephone links also make it possible for one computer to be linked to a large number of terminals. Many companies need to use a computer but do not have enough work to justify buying one. So they rent space on a large machine from a computer bureau. The terminal enables them to input and output from the computer whenever they want. The computer itself may handle many different kinds of information from many different companies, storing it all in its memory.

Other kinds of terminal include graphics tablets that enable drawings to be fed into the computer. A plotter with a roll of paper and a pen produces output in the form of drawings. A few computers can read typescript. Some can recognize and take orders from the human voice, although they only understand a very small vocabulary. And some can even say a few words.

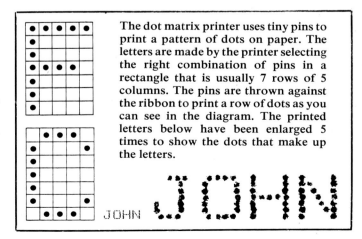

The dot matrix printer uses tiny pins to print a pattern of dots on paper. The letters are made by the printer selecting the right combination of pins in a rectangle that is usually 7 rows of 5 columns. The pins are thrown against the ribbon to print a row of dots as you can see in the diagram. The printed letters below have been enlarged 5 times to show the dots that make up the letters.

Computer Games

Space Invaders, Pac-man, Asteroids are names known all over the world. They are the names of electronic games that have one thing in common – they all have tiny computers inside them, controlled by silicon chips.

Much of the very complicated electronics that grew up in the late 1970s – electronics developed for the computer and space industries – are now being used in our electronic games.

By 1975, integrated circuits were getting smaller and more powerful. Complicated electronic circuits could be produced quite cheaply on tiny silicon chips. So, along came the video game.

Today's video game has at its heart a microprocessor. The plug-in cartridges contain complicated computer programs which operate the microprocessor and make the game on the video screen. To produce a new game, someone must write a new program to control the microprocessor.

Any spot on the video screen can be made to glow by the programmer typing in numbers which tell the computer to light up a spot so many lines from the top of the screen and the time from the start of that line. This point of light (which can of course be in one of several colors) can be repeated in various places and for various periods of time. By doing this, patches of brightness in any shape or color can be built on the screen.

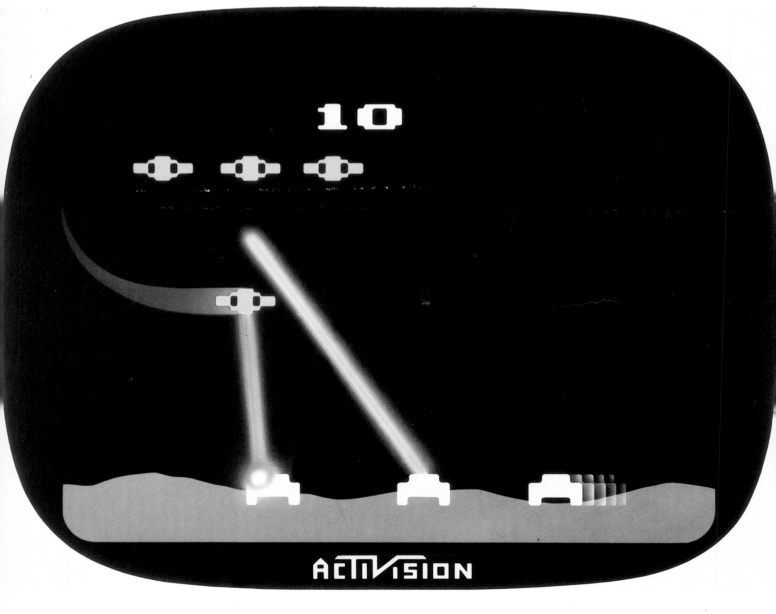

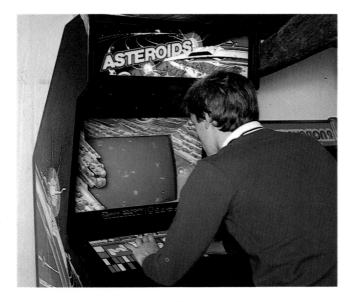

Board Games

The microprocessor is also at the center of many different board games – chess, bridge, backgammon etc. These games allow us to test our skill against the program which has been built into the machines.

Early computer chess games were rather crude. But the electronic circuits have been improved so much that today's chess machines are a match for almost anyone. Usually the player can decide how difficult the game will be to win. This choice of difficulty controls the number of choices the computer will look at before it makes its move. This means that the time taken for the computer to make a move can vary enormously. In a simple beginner-level game, the computer will make its move almost immediately. In some very advanced games the computer may sometimes "think" about a move for three or four hours. Some computer chess programs let the computer examine ten or more moves ahead. Although computers work at a fantastic speed, it still takes time to examine all the millions of possibilities that are possible in a few moves on a chess board.

Some chess games have a special sensory board on which the pieces are placed. In these games, the microprocessor knows where all the pieces are at any time.

Above: Some arcade games use special effects, including many sounds, to make the game exciting.
Below: You can play games such as chess on a microcomputer by plugging in a prerecorded program from a cassette or cartridge. With a cartridge, you just slot it in. Cassettes have to be loaded into the computer by playing them through a cassette recorder.
Below right: Some chess games can even speak their moves to you.

The Computer Can Draw Too

One of the most exciting jobs the computer can be made to do is to draw. A new kind of art is growing up. The computer terminal and the television screen are taking the place of the drawing board.

A graphics tablet is a flat board on which we can draw with a special stylus. As lines are drawn on the tablet, they appear as though by magic on the television screen in front of us. Simple graphics are used to make designs, maps and graphs. These can be stored in the computer's memory for future use.

Large-scale Graphics

With large computers it is possible to produce really complicated color images of characters, machines, buildings or any kind of shape in three dimensions. There are programs to produce surfaces of different colors and textures. And we can look at the model from any angle as the computer is told to turn it around on the screen, bring it closer or push it further away. We can even get the computer to "light" the object from any angle in any color.

There are different systems for making color graphics, but they all divide up the screen into a series of dots, or *pixels*, along each line on the screen. (One system has, for example, 1024 pixels on each of the 574 lines that make up the picture.) Each pixel can light up in any of 64 colors.

Computer-drawing a Cartoon Film

Animating a cartoon film used to be a long, expensive business. In a full length cartoon there might have been a quarter of a million individual drawings, all done by hand. These drawings were put on film and passed through the film camera at a speed of 24 pictures every second. This gave the impression of movement.

Now the animator works with a computer and an electronic drawing board. The artist can touch the surface of the board with an electronic pen to make colored marks appear on the TV screen. He can "paint" on the screen and instruct the computer to change the drawing slightly to the next image he needs. He can touch an area with his pen and select a certain color. The computer will fill in that area with the color the artist wants.

Above and right: Scientists and engineers are using computers to help them test their designs before the machines are built. This saves a great deal of time and money.
Right center: The computer can show us in a realistic way what a shape will look like from different angles. Computer design is becoming more and more important in industry.
Far right: Examples of computer-aided cartoons. Note the sound track on one edge.
Below: A computer design produced by a matrix printer.

The result of this cooperation between artist and computer is much quicker animation and the creation of smoother, more real-looking images. And all this is stored in the computer's memory to be recalled at any time.

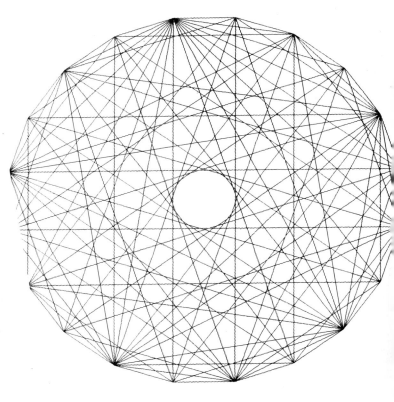

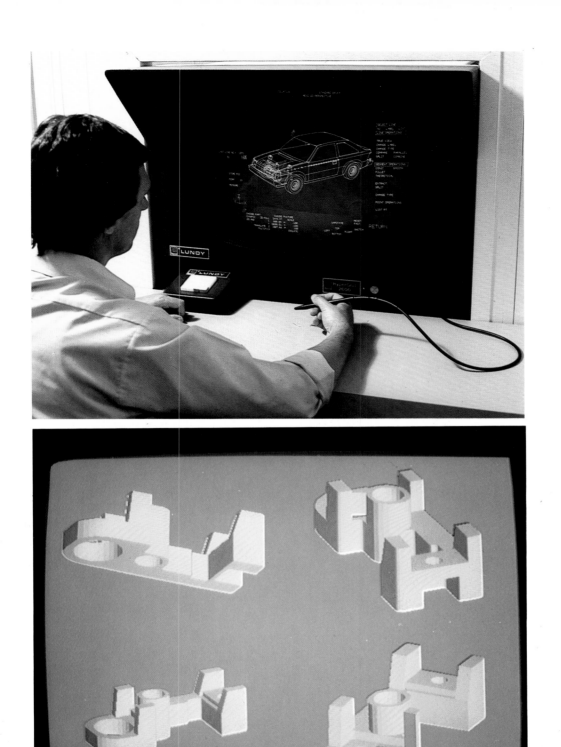
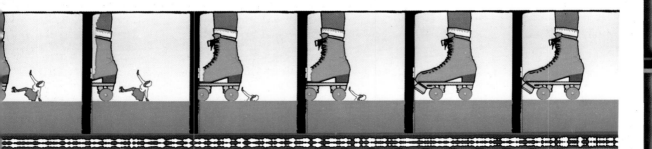

Flying on the Ground

Many aircraft can now take off and land entirely by computer. But aircrew are still vitally important, and they can now be trained to handle these complex machines without leaving the ground.

Computers are being used everywhere – on land, at sea and in the air. One of their most useful jobs is in helping to make flying safer. One new aircraft, the Boeing 757, is now completely computerized. The control panels in the cockpit show all the information the pilot needs in full color on cathode ray tubes.

Computers in the aircraft keep a check on the plane's performance during flight and display the results on cathode ray tubes in front of each pilot's seat. These screens show the aircraft's course, rate of climb or descent, the horizon angle, wind speed and the angle it is coming from, distance to go to the plane's destination and many other items.

The computers also keep a check on the two engines and other systems, giving warning if anything is not exactly as it should be. In addition, the flight crews can ask the computers for information as to the best rate of climb when taking off and the take-off distance.

Flying on the Ground

The computer is also now playing a vital part in training pilots to fly airliners such as the 757. Companies that fly the aircraft have *flight simulators* on the ground which are exactly the same as the aircraft's cockpit. All the instruments are the same and when a pilot is being trained to use them the controls feel exactly as they would in

Above: The Boeing 757 cockpit is completely computerized. The pilot can select the information to be viewed on his cathode ray tube display.
Right: Two views of the Boeing 737 flight simulator. The pilots are far away from any airfield and the scene around them is entirely computer generated. All the controls act exactly as they would on a real flight, and the scene outside can be changed from day to dusk or night.

real flight. What the pilot sees through the cockpit windows is also created by computers. Perhaps it is an exact image of what it is like to land at LA International Airport or what it feels like to take off from Kennedy, New York. And the instructor can change the conditions to night flying, fog or dusk at the throw of a switch.

It is important that the computers respond exactly as a real aircraft would to whatever the pilot does. The motion of the flight simulator is produced by a hydraulic power unit. This can move the cabin in any direction at the computer's command. So it is possible for the pilot to feel what it is like to taxi along an icy runway, fly through bumpy cloud formations or bang down to a not-too-perfect landing.

Flight simulators have many uses. They train pilots who are changing from one aircraft type to another; they are used in upgrading pilots from first officer to captain, and they train crews on routes which are new to them. It has been said that you can now fly an aircraft from LA to New York without ever leaving the ground. Simulators are also used by the world's air forces in training pilots in front-line tactics.

Above: The computer has generated this image of what it is like to land a helicopter on an oil platform at sea.
Below: This is what a simulator is like from the outside.

Robots

Robots have several advantages over human beings when they have been programmed to do certain jobs. They can, if necessary, work without stopping for 24 hours a day. They can work in places where a human worker could not survive. They very seldom get sick. They never ask for more money or go on strike. For these and other reasons, robots are changing the face of many industries.

Every day that passes sees more and more robots going about their tasks in factories all over the world. They weld things together, they spray paint, they load and unload. They handle hot metal castings and are even taking their place alongside human workers in assembly lines. But none of these robot workers looks at all like the robots in science fiction. They are very complex machines.

What is a Robot?

Automatic machines have been working in factories for many years, but they are not robots. So, what is a robot? A robot is a machine that can be programmed to do different tasks. And most people think that a robot must also have an arm of some kind that can be made to do work for us. Once a robot has been programmed, its master is a computer.

Why Robots?

Why are robots beginning to replace human workers in many factories? There are several reasons. Once they have been correctly programmed, robots are better than humans at certain tasks. They are stronger, being able to lift and handle heavy objects. They don't get tired or bored. Switch them on and they go on working accurately for as long as they are needed. And they can work in dangerous, hot, noisy or dirty places that are impossible for human workers to tolerate.

Teaching the Robot

The robot is usually programmed by the person who will supervise it and who knows about the job the robot will do.

If the robot has to be programmed to pick something up and put it down somewhere else, the programmer holds a *teach unit* attached to the robot's arm. The teach unit has buttons that drive each of the robot's joints. As the programmer slowly presses buttons to guide the robot arms in the direction he wants it to go, he also keeps pressing a record button as the arm goes from position to position. This enters each position into the robot's computer memory. When the whole movement is complete, the robot can then carry out the task on its own. Trial runs of the program may show the need for small adjustments to the movement until it is just right.

The robot may be made to do a completely different job on the following month. But the

Above: Robots spot welding and assembling cars. Very careful programming is needed to make the assembly line run smoothly when robots and other machines work closely like this.

Right: The film *Star Wars* brought two new robot stars to the screen – C-3PO and R2-D2. Science is still a very long way from being able to make machines with the intelligence of these two characters.

THE THREE LAWS OF ROBOTICS

Perhaps the person who has done most to make us think about robots is the scientist and science fiction writer Isaac Asimov. In a series of stories published in the 1940s he wrote about the Three Laws of Robotics. All robots were to be built according to these laws:
1. Robots must not injure a human being or allow a human being to come to harm.
2. A robot must obey orders given to it by human beings, except where such orders would conflict with the First Law.
3. A robot must protect itself, as long as such protection does not conflict with the First or Second Laws.

memory of the picking up and putting down task is still in the computer's memory and the robot can come back to that job at any time.

A Smoother Movement

The kind of programming described above is called point-to-point. This kind of program is used for things like spot welding as well as for moving things about. The robot moves in a rather jerky fashion.

Sometimes a smoother movement is needed. For smooth movements such as paint spraying, the best human painter in the factory actually leads the robot spray head in the path that is required. Once the program has been worked out and corrected, the robot will paint exactly as the expert painter would do the job.

Remote Control in Space

In 1976, two American Viking spacecraft landed on Mars. There were no human beings in these craft. The craft were controlled by computers on board and by radio from Earth. The main task of the Vikings was to find out if any kind of life was present on the Red Planet.

Each Viking was in two parts – an orbiter and a lander. The orbiter kept on circling the planet while the lander separated and touched down on its three spindly legs. The orbiter acted as a radio

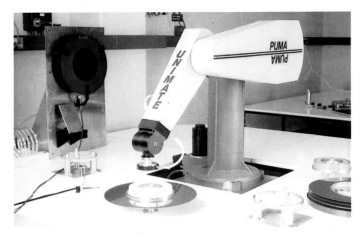

Above: A robot arm assembling computer disks. A task such as this requires very accurate movement.

relay station between the lander and Earth. It also had cameras to take pictures of the planet and instruments to detect water and measure temperatures.

The lander was a mass of instruments that measured temperature, wind speed, atmospheric pressure and took pictures of its surroundings. Most important, it had a robot-like arm that scooped up soil and allowed instruments on board to test it for signs of life. All these experiments were controlled by a computer on board, and this computer could be controlled from Earth as required.

RADIO WAVES TAKE TIME

One of the problems of remote control in space is the time it takes radio signals to get there and back. Communicating with astronauts on the Moon wasn't too difficult because radio waves can get to the Moon in 1.3 seconds. But if people ever land on Mars it will be different. Mars is about 49 million miles (78 million km) from Earth. Even traveling at the fantastic speed of 186,000 miles (300,000 km) per second, it takes radio signals nearly $4\frac{1}{2}$ minutes to cover the distance. It therefore took $4\frac{1}{2}$ minutes for an Earth command to reach the Viking craft. This will mean that if we ever ask an astronaut on Mars a question, we will have to wait nearly 9 minutes before we get an answer.

The Viking probes which landed on Mars had mechanical arms. These arms scooped up Martian soil, tested it and radioed information about it back to Earth. The probes found no sign of life on Mars.

Unfortuntely, neither Viking craft was able to detect any sign of living things in the Martian soil.

Robots of the Future

Robots are already taking over from humans in some factories. As years go by, people will almost disappear from assembly lines, their places being taken by accurately programmed robots.

Future robots will be given a simple vision system. This will allow them to choose different courses of action, depending on what they see.

Many will also have a sense of touch. This will stop them from damaging things by gripping too hard or from letting things fall when they don't hold them hard enough. Robots might even be given a sense that we humans don't have. They could be fitted with proximity sensors. These would let the robot feel how close it is to something. This would prevent it bumping into other robots or people.

Robots in the Home

Although robots are taking over in the factory, it is difficult to see how they could ever fit into our homes. As we all know, homes are not organized places like assembly lines in factories, where the same thing keeps happening time after time. How could we ever train a robot to vacuum the floor if we humans left papers, books and coffee cups on it? How would the robot know what to throw out?

Perhaps some day, however, we will have pet robots. These could be programmed to hold simple conversations with their owners. And, of course, they could do all sorts of things that computers are learning to do: play games, sing songs and tell stories. It is rather doubtful, however, whether man's best friend will ever be his computer.

Learning with Computers

As time goes by, more and more educational aids are being used in the classroom. Calculators, video recorders, overhead projectors and language laboratories are all in regular use. Now comes the microcomputer, a machine that is spreading through education like wildfire.

People are saying that by the end of this century, every school desk in developed countries will have a microcomputer on it. Whether this will happen or not, it is certainly true that the use of micros in schools is increasing at a fantastic rate.

Learning to Program

A child who can program a computer has two advantages. Firstly, he or she is at home with the machine which will be a big part of life in the 21st century. Secondly, programming leads to a new kind of straightforward thinking that will serve him or her well in many other ways.

"Computer literacy" – learning how to make computers work for you – is a skill that will soon be as important a part of our education as learning to add and subtract. And there is only one way to learn how to program: to actually do it, to sit at a keyboard and try things out for oneself. Working a computer is called "hands-on" experience.

Experiments have shown that young primary school children can quickly learn to put together simple programs in BASIC or whatever computer language they have been taught.

Computers are now more attractive than they used to be. Color graphics can produce charts, diagrams, cartoon characters and all kinds of things. The graphics can be produced on a graphics tablet. This is a flat board with a special pointed instrument called a stylus, which is like a pen. As you put the end of the stylus on the board, a dot of light appears on the VDU screen. Dotted points can be joined with perfect lines, and pictures can be moved about on the screen.

Computer-Assisted Learning

Computers can also be used to teach people who know nothing about programming. One of the first and simplest computer teaching machines was Speak and Spell. This machine, not much bigger than a pocket calculator, stores about 240 words in its memory. The computer actually speaks the word it wants you to spell. You type on the keyboard how you think the word is spelled. If you are right, the machine praises you and speaks another word. If you are wrong, you are given two more tries before the machine gives the right answer.

Now, many much more complicated programs are available. With the aid of newer, more complex programs you can teach yourself anything from a foreign language to the game of bridge.

Learning at Home and in School

The connection of a microcomputer to the telephone system in your home or school allows you to connect with a vast amount of information. In the U.S., transmission of educational programs over the telephone lines is under way. Control Data's Plato network contains 8,000 to 10,000 hours of instruction, including basic skills through grade 12, data processing, random lessons and games. It can be used by the Apple Microcomputer, the IBM Personal Computer, the Control Data 110 and the Zenith 100.

Below: Children are finding out that learning can be fun on a computer.

Above: Today's computers can produce all kinds of colors.
Above right: In geometry class the computer helps you to work out shapes and angles.

Below: Working with a graphics board. When the outline of the map of Australia is traced with the special pen, it appears on the screen.

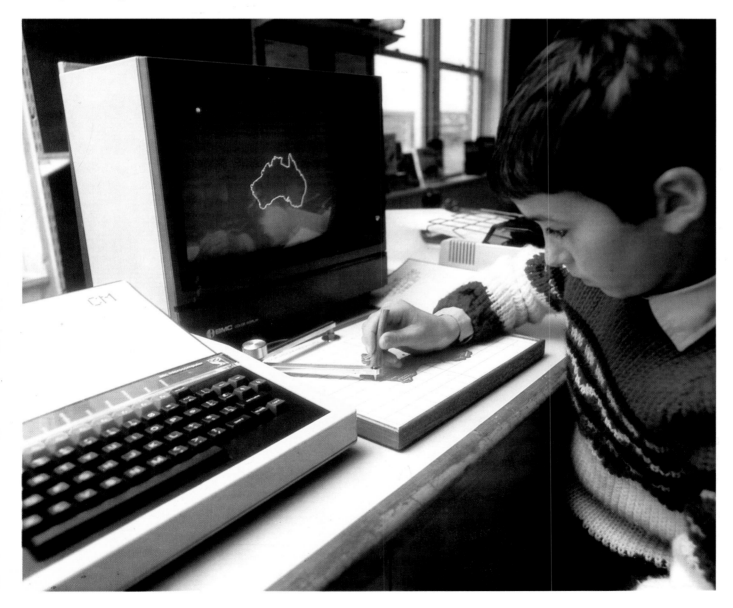

Computers and the Police

The best way to make sure that crime does not grow is to increase the chances of criminals being caught. The task of tracking down criminals is made easier by rapid communications and the use of computers.

One use for the computer that is becoming more and more important is in the fight against crime. The silicon chip is helping police forces all over the world to catch thieves and track down criminals who in the past would have escaped detection.

Checking Car Numbers

A television camera linked to a computer can be placed at some point along a highway where vehicles stop to pay tolls or stop for some other reason. As the camera records the license plates of vehicles in as many as six lanes of traffic, the numbers are fed automatically to the computer.

The computer, within seconds, compares the numbers with perhaps 100,000 numbers of stolen vehicles which have been programmed into its memory. If one of the numbers picked up by the camera corresponds to one of the stolen car plates, the computer sounds a warning and shows the number. Within seconds a police car will be stopping the car for questioning.

Scientists are now trying to design a camera that

This police computer system holds details of thousands of fingerprints. In a few seconds it will match any of these with those of a suspect.

The vaults in banks are now covered by electronic equipment.

will photograph car license plates while the vehicles are moving. The police would then be able to set up cameras on busy roads so that these roads can be checked continuously.

Fingerprinting

Another use for the computer in police work is in identifying fingerprints. Each of us has fingerprints that are different from everyone else's in the whole world. The checking of fingerprints is therefore a valuable means of detecting people who have committed crimes.

But the task of actually comparing a suspect's fingerprints with the thousands held by a large police force is a rather tedious one. This is where the computer comes in. It is now possible to program a computer to hold details of the fingerprints of half a million people. In a few seconds the computer will match any of these prints with those of a suspect.

Computer Detectives

Police computers are fed with all kinds of details about people who have been criminals or who have associated with criminals. The computer is brilliant at fitting together small pieces of information that may point to a suspect.

One case will serve as an example of what the computer can do. A woman saw two suspicious looking men coming out of a building at night. As they passed her she heard one of them speak with an unusual regional accent. The same man had a tattoo mark on his face.

The next day, newspaper reports told of a burglary at the building in question and the woman went to the police. The two small pieces of information and an approximate age were fed into the computer. Within seconds the machine had sorted out three names from the thousands in its memory. One of the three men was arrested.

Security Systems

In addition to its work with the police, the computer now plays a vital part in making business premises secure against theft, fire and other dangers.

In one modern system, a central computer is controlled by a single operator. There are sensors at intervals all over the building, each connected to the computer. These sensors monitor intruders, fire and smoke, as well as employees who have every right to be there. The computer is not fooled if a wire is cut. It immediately raises an alarm.

If anything odd happens, the computer works out what kind of action to take. If there is a fire, it automatically switches on sprinkler systems in the right part of the building. It can open or lock doors. It can switch on lights so that an intruder can be seen on a television screen. It can also show a plan of the area where trouble has been detected.

Special Systems

In some buildings, special precautions have to be taken against theft and sabotage. The building to be protected is partitioned off into zones. These zones have electrically controlled doors which can only be opened by people with special magnetic cards that look like credit cards. The cards can be different for each zone so that certain people can only get into certain parts of the building. When the correct card is put into a slot, the door opens for a few seconds. As a card is put into the slot, the computer checks the number on it.

There is even a security system that recognizes people's fingerprints. Before someone can get through a door, he has to have his fingerprints compared automatically with a set held by the computer.

Bank vaults are becoming more and more secure against theft. Some are fitted with special sensors that set off an alarm when they are tampered with. They can be linked to a computer that can recognize when the doors are being touched by someone who shouldn't be doing so.

Other Detectors

Another security system is worked by microwave detectors. These high frequency waves are used to scan large areas such as factory floors or large offices. As soon as someone walks through the microwave beam, an alarm sounds.

Ultrasonic sound waves are also used. (These sound waves are so high that they cannot be heard by the human ear.) The waves are reflected off walls and pieces of equipment to produce a certain pattern. Should this pattern be broken by someone walking anywhere in the area, the alarm is sounded.

This computerized security system allows one man to monitor a whole building. Various areas can be covered by the TV screens.

Computers and Television

As more and more homes have their own microcomputer it is becoming possible to link them with the outside world via the telephone system. Your home micro will one day draw on all the information stored in vast databanks anywhere in the world.

Television sets can be used to receive news and information of all kinds coming from a central computer. The information can reach your televison set in two ways. It can be transmitted with the normal television signal and picked up by your TV antenna. But your television set must be specially adapted to receive it. This system is called Teletext.

The other system, called Videotex, is quite different. This system sends the information along telephone lines. The signals have to be decoded (turned from analogue into digital signals) by a special unit called a modem before your television set can turn them into pictures and words.

Teletext

Teletext is exactly what its name suggests. The "text" – that is, the information put out – is broadcast at the same time as ordinary TV

Below: Part of the index to information that Teletext suscribers can key into their television screen.

programs. This information is not just words and figures. It can also be graphics and illustrations.

Every image that appears on your television screen is broadcast as a series of lines. But in fact the TV picture does not use up all the lines that are available. A number are left spare. Teletext uses some of these spare lines.

What happens is this. An editorial team types in information in the form of pages into a computer. Each page is 24 lines deep, 40 characters (letters, figures and spaces) wide and can appear in several colors. The information in each page is coded by the computer and broadcast at the same time as normal programs. The pages are sent out one after another at quarter-second intervals.

To receive Teletext, your TV set must have a decoder. You can select any page you want to see by push buttons.

Teletext broadcasts include news and sports results, weather and traffic information, stock market updates, music and film reviews, jokes, games, puzzles and more.

Teletext began in Britain in 1974, and variations spread to France, Canada and other countries.

Several Teletext systems are planned or in operation in the United States and Canada. Time Incorporated offers a full channel sent along cable TV lines. And both NBC and CBS have Teletext systems. However, the decoder needed for these is expensive and is not yet built into TV sets, so audiences are still quite small. In Canada, a system called Telidon combines Teletext with Videotex technology. As of mid-1982, four commercial Telidon services were in operation.

Videotex

Videotex differs from Teletext in several important ways. The link from the central computer to your television screen is via the telephone system. The information provided is very much greater, and Videotex is a two-way service. Users can call up the pages they want by pressing any one of about 200,000 page numbers on a special adapter linked to their own telephones. They can also use the service to make hotel and travel reservations and so on.

As in Teletext, the pages you call up appear on your television screen. But, as the information is sent along the telephone network, when you are

using Videotex your telephone line is busy. If you know which page you want, you can call it up direct. Otherwise you use a complicated series of indexes to find exactly the information you require.

In the United States, Videotex is still developing. There are, however, several Videotex services planned or already in operation across the country. Time Incorporated offers a service providing information and computer games. Subscribers to another service called The Source can get almost anything from stock reports and government news, to sports scores and information on hobbies and pets. They can follow a soap opera, reserve an airline ticket, play a Star Trek game, or make a restaurant reservation. As more and more people acquire a home computer – and there are about two million American users today – Videotex may well become part of the American way of life. By the 1990s you may be able to do all your shopping from home, buying the goods through the computer and using it to pay for them from your bank account.

Above: A Videotex service comes to your television screen over the telephone line.

Below: A Videotex service can be used to make hotel and travel reservations.

Banking by Computer

As everyone knows, banking is big business. Huge amounts of money are handled every day. It is big business in another way too. The banks have to cope with an enormous number of transactions. And banks have to do far more than just process checks.

Even the simplest banking transaction has to be recorded carefully and accurately. You decide to give me a present of $100 and write me a check, which I pay in at the local branch of my bank. My account must now be credited with $100, and yours has to be debited with the same amount. In other words, $100 has to be transferred from your account to mine.

Transferring money like this means that a great deal of information has to be passed around. (Remember that nearly all financial deals take place on paper only. Actual money in bills and coin seldom move about.)

Writing a Check

Take a look at a check. At the bottom are three sets of figures printed in magnetic ink. These represent the sorting code of the bank branch; the number of the customer's account; and the check number, which is unique to that account. When it reads these numbers, the computer can automatically identify which of the bank's hundreds of thousands of customers wrote that particular check.

What happens, then, when I pay in your check for $100? You have already written the amount payable in words and figures. A special machine is used to record the same information in magnetic ink on the bottom of the check. Along with thousands of others, the check is then sent to the bank's head office. Each bank exchanges checks with its competitors, so that they each land up with just the checks issued to its customers.

Then the document-processors get to work. These computerized machines can handle as many as 100,000 items every hour. They sort all the checks into separate piles for each branch. Then the computer reads each check and records the account number, the check number and the amount on magnetic disk. The next day, the checks themselves are returned to the branch from which they were issued. At the same time, the

information on disk is fed into another computer which holds details of each branch's accounts. This computer automatically updates individual customers' accounts; in this case it deducts $100 from your account.

SWIFT

This is the name for a system for transferring money electronically from one country to another. (The initials stand for Society for Worldwide Interbank Financial Telecommunication.) Nearly a thousand different banks in forty countries in many parts of the world belong. Computers and telecommunications networks – mainly telephone links and communications satellites – are used to make and receive payments. These transfers take a very short time indeed to complete. This is very important in world finance, since a lot depends on buying and selling at exactly the right moment.

Machines That Offer Cash

Customers of most major banks can now get cash from a machine – without having to write a check.

The machine is in fact a computer terminal and keyboard, linked directly to the bank's central computer, which has details of every customer's account. Customers are issued with a magnetically coded plastic card. The code on the card contains information about their account number and the branch at which it is held. Customers are also given a personal number.

What happens when you want cash is this. You

Most banks now have computer-controlled machines from which customers can obtain cash at any time of day or night.

76

Above: A new kind of banking. The cashier has a computer terminal on her side of the counter. She punches in details of what the customer wants. When the customer has checked this, he punches in his own personal identification number on a small keyboard on his side of the counter (below). There is no paperwork.

Into the Future

Before long, you may be able to do all your major shopping with cards like this. Some stores already have cashdesk terminals. Instead of paying with money or by check, you will hand over a plastic card encoded with information about your bank account. The terminal reads the details on the card, and the cashier keys in the amount you have spent. All this information goes to the bank's central computers, which check that you have enough funds to pay for what you have bought. Then you key in your personal number on a special customer keyboard. Your account is immediately debited, that is, the cost of the goods subtracted; the store's account is at the same time credited with the same amount – and you walk off with your purchases.

The customer's personal number is very important in these systems. It guarantees his security. Even if his card is stolen, it cannot be used. No one else knows the customer's number.

To install a complex network of terminals in every store and shop throughout the country would cost a great deal of money. It may be a long time before terminals like these are found even in every large supermarket and department store. But when they are, we will be well on the way to becoming a cashless society.

Some modern banks no longer have counter screens separating the customer from the cashier. Vacuum tubes whisk money away to a separate area and time-lock tills are used to provide customers with cash.

feed your card into the machine, which automatically reads the information coded on it and transmits that information to the central computer. On the keyboard you type in your personal number and the amount of money you want. This information too is sent to the central computer. The computer checks it – making sure that your personal number tallies with the information on the card. It also checks that there is enough money in the account before instructing the terminal to make the payment. All this only takes about half a minute, and then you get your card back and the money you asked for.

At some machines you can also pay money in and find out how much you have in your bank account.

Less and Less Paper

People who work in offices will be – and are being – the first to feel the effects of the computer revolution. These lightning-fast machines are taking over in all kinds of ways.

When you walk into most offices, what is the first thing you will see? Almost certainly it will be paper – paper in typewriters, on desks, in filing cabinets, on drawing boards and on bookshelves.

Walk into an up-to-date high-technology office, however, and the last thing you will discover is paper. Desks have become work stations equipped with microcomputers, their keyboards and visual display units. Electronic typewriters have taken the place of the old fashioned electric machines, and there will be word processors.

The Office Revolution

The big revolution that first computers and then micro-processors have brought about is this: they have separated figures and words from paper. Records of all kinds are vital in business and industry. You have to keep a record of the agreements you have made, the salaries you pay people, the sales you achieve. And there is a need

Above: In today's office the word processor is becoming a vitally important tool.
Below: People no longer have to fly vast distances to have a meeting. Here businessmen in different parts of the world meet via the television screen. This is called videoconferencing.

to keep accounts to show how well or badly your business is doing.

Until recently, all these records had to be kept on paper; there was nothing else on which you could store them. And every time you wanted to update or alter them, you had to write or type them out again.

There have been two main stages in the office revolution. From about the late 1950s onwards, more and more large companies installed big mainframe computers – number crunchers as they are often called. These did number work of all kinds. They dealt with salaries, produced accounts, handled the control of stock, and did many other similar jobs.

It was the microprocessor that brought about the second stage of the revolution. Along with changes in telecommunications, they have completely changed the way we process and transmit information.

Microcomputers are small and cheap. Everyone can use them, not just computer specialists locked away in separate computer rooms. You can call up sales figures and examine them on the screen on your desk. You can draft a report on a word processor and correct and edit it as you go along –

or alter it later. And you can do all this without handling a single piece of paper.

Sending and Receiving Words and Pictures

People have been able to talk over long distances and send cables and telex messages for many years. Now, however, modern electronic equipment can send not just conversations but words, figures and images of all kinds to anywhere in the world.

The key to all this is *digitization* – the 0s and 1s of the binary system. As we have seen, computers process information by coding it in the binary system as 0s and 1s. The new telecomunications equipment also handles information in this form. So if you want to send a document to a colleague in, say, the Tokyo branch of your company, you simply type it into your computer, which translates it into a sequence of binary numbers. These then enter the telecommunications network and are transmitted to Tokyo, probably by satellite. When the binary signals reach your colleague's computer, they get translated back into ordinary words and figures and appear on his VDU screen.

Things are Changing

In practice, how paperless your office is likely to be depends on the kind of work you do. People in

The room below holds as much information in its computer disks as several large libraries.

Many firms still have typing pools where rows of people type letters – often the same letter to different addresses. But if you want to send the same letter to hundreds of different people, all you have to do is type it once on a word processor. The letter is then stored in the computer's memory and repeated with any address you give the machine.

commerce – banking, finance, insurance and so on – are already using the new electronic office technology a great deal. And thousands of offices, large, medium and small, are letting computers take over the routine work.

But the hardware is costly. And often it can take quite a long time, and therefore money, to write software programs that do exactly what you want them to do. People have to be retrained to use the new equipment. Some jobs are lost – particularly among typists, secretaries, clerks and so on, the people who had to do the routine paper work.

Often the new technology will release these people to do more interesting and more creative work. Managers and executives will also have to change their work style. The whole point of the new technology is that you find the information

Office telephone switchboards are changing too. This is a recent electronic model.

you need yourself. Instead of asking a filing clerk or your secretary to look something up in a file, you do it yourself on your computer terminal. This means that many managers who have no idea how to use a typewriter will have to learn to use a keyboard.

Teleordering

Teleordering is a good example of the way computer systems can be useful in small businesses.

At any time there are thousands and thousands of books in print – adventure stories, schoolbooks, novels, biographies – books on every subject under the sun. There are so many that no bookstore can hope to stock more than a tiny fraction of these.

So quite a lot of the time booksellers have to order a book specially for a customer. And of course they have to restock popular books – the latest paperback novel that everyone wants to read – and they have to make sure they have the steady sellers in stock: dictionaries, cook books, gardening books, guidebooks and so on.

Ordering is quite a complex business, especially since there are hundreds of different publishers in the country. You have to fill in the publisher's order form, giving the name of the author, the title of the book, and the ISBN number. (ISBN stands for International Standard Book Number. It is a number given to every single title. You can see the ISBN number of this book on the page that faces the title.)

Ordering by Computer

Teleordering cuts out a great deal of the routine work involved in ordering stock. The bookseller has to buy a small computer terminal consisting of a keyboard and a VDU screen. The central computer of the whole system holds in its memory a detailed record of every book in print, including its author, title, price and ISBN.

Once the bookseller's terminal has been installed, the procedure is simple. At quiet moments during the day, or after he has closed for the night, the bookseller inputs all the orders taken. These are stored in the computer's memory. During the night the central computer calls up each terminal in turn on a telephone line and extracts the orders stored there.

The central computer then sorts and processes each batch of orders. It finds the author, title and price of each book, and then lists each shop's order to each publisher. The orders are then sent out to the different publishers the same night, either directly into their computer or in the form of a printout on paper. A record of its orders is also sent back to each bookshop, ready for the start of the next working day.

Ordering by computer brings many advantages. It cuts out most of the paperwork and produces clearer records. Orders are fulfilled more quickly and more accurately. If a book is out of print the customer can be informed more quickly. Staff have to spend less time messing around with pieces of paper and so can spend more time selling books.

This girl is feeding the day's orders into the teleordering computer. During the night the orders will be processed automatically.

Computers and Airlines

Computer systems are vital to the successful running of an airline. They are used in every part of its operations. As a passenger you are most likely to come into contact with them when you book a seat and when you arrive at the airport for your flight.

Departure Control

Getting a plane off the ground and on its way is a complicated business. It is not simply a matter of making sure that all the passengers are on board, loading their baggage, and telling the captain to take off. Aircraft have to be loaded very carefully. It is not only the total weight – of the aircraft itself, passengers and crew, their baggage, cargo and fuel – that is important. For a safe flight, the load must be properly distributed throughout the plane.

Almost the whole process is computer-controlled. It starts two or three days before the flight, when the flight is "created." This involves setting up a "passenger record," which consists of information about each passenger.

When you arrive at the airport, you check in at a check-in desk. The clerk types your name on his computer keyboard, and the computer checks it against the passenger record. This enables a continuous check to be kept on the number of passengers still to arrive for the flight. The computer also records either the weight of your baggage or the number of pieces you have with you.

At about the same time as the check-in opens the computer sends an "offer" of space to the cargo center. The center holds freight items waiting for space on a flight.

Loading the Plane

The computer's next main task is to issue the load plan. This is sent to the ramp loading area, where the holds of the plane are actually loaded. The load plan shows exactly where in the hold baggage and cargo should be placed.

About 10 to 20 minutes before take-off, when passenger check-in is just closing, the computer issues the load sheet. This is an official international document that every captain must see before take-off. It lists passengers and their destinations, and cargo (including "funny" cargo such as live animals).

Imagine what it would be like trying to run a big airline without computers!

Reading Machines

Most children can read fairly well by the time they are 6 or 7. But thousands of clever scientists have been struggling for years to make a machine that can read nearly as well as a 6-year-old. And they have not yet succeeded.

Look at the examples on the left and you can begin to see the problems facing a reading machine. The characters in each line are completely different, but we can recognize the words without any difficulty. No machine, no matter how complicated and expensive, can yet read all the examples. Human beings seem to have a wonderful capacity for recognizing printed or written characters. But how we manage to do it is not exactly known. Our brains seem to learn to recognize the shapes of characters, no matter how out of shape they are. Reading machines have to be slowly and painstakingly programmed to learn how to recognize them.

How do Machines Do It?

To recognize the shape of a character, a reading machine scans it with a laser scanner, a group of photo cells or a television camera. The character is represented in the machine as a pattern of binary bits. The machine compares the pattern with patterns that have been programmed into it. When the machine compares the two patterns, it counts the bits that differ. If the number of differing bits is less than a certain number, the machine is satisfied that it has recognized the character.

Machines are still a long way behind humans in recognizing script handwriting. Some very complicated machines can recognize hand-written block capitals, provided there are spaces between the letters.

Above: This machine reads the magnetic ink characters on checks and sorts them at a rate of 2500 a minute.

Sorting Checks

Millions of checks are written every day. All these have to be sorted and sent to the banks of the people who write them. It is impossible to sort all these checks by hand, so machines have been designed to do the job. Checks have special characters printed in magnetic ink along the bottom edge. Machines can read these characters (usually figures) and use the information they contain to work fast sorting equipment that sends the checks to their right destinations.

Above: This automatic sorting machine sorts letters after phosphorescent dots have been added to them. A scanner reads the dots on the envelope and sends the letter into the right box.

Postal Sorting

Many countries now use automatic postal sorting. There are several ways of doing this. In the U.S. and Japan, machines actually read the postcodes on the envelopes. These machines control mechanical sorters which automatically put each letter in its correct pigeon hole for dispatch. In the Japanese system, the reading machines reject about 8 percent of letters because they cannot read the post codes. Those 8 percent are put aside by the machine and have to be sorted by hand.

In some countries, a postman reads the address as envelopes pass in front of him. He types the post codes on a special machine that automatically sorts the envelopes.

Other Reading Machines

There are many different kinds of reading machines. The cost of a machine depends on two main things – the range of characters that have to be read and the speed at which they have to be read.

If the paper, the ink and the type of print are exactly what a particular machine has been designed for, most machines will have very few failures. But the slightest smudge of a character throws the reading machine out completely. It may, for example, mistake an l for a 1 or a capital I, or a 5 for an S. If the machine has to recognize only numbers, then the print quality does not have to be as good.

The full value of machine reading is found in cases such as the journalist who types his story directly on to a typewriter that produces very good, clear type that has been specially selected for a particular reading machine. The machine can then read the journalist's story directly into a computer-typesetting machine that produces actual printed words. This system does away with the need for someone to retype the journalist's story into the typesetting machine.

Reading Lines

A much cheaper method of machine reading is a system that requires the machine to read parallel thin and thick lines rather than letters and numbers. This system is being used more and more in supermarkets and libraries. (If you look on the back cover of this book you will see what is called a bar code.) A laser pen is passed over the bar code. The pen reads the information which goes to a computer. This information, which includes the price of the item, is used at checkouts and also to keep a record of sales.

Reading Machines of the Future

It will probably be many years before reading machines will be anywhere near as good as our human senses. But as more and more words and figures are typed into computers it is becoming more important that better reading machines be designed.

Perhaps we will only be able to make the really efficient machine when we find out how our brains manage to recognize instantly all kinds of characters that to us are the same but to the machine look entirely different. One thing is certain: when this reading machine is produced, it will read at speeds that we will find quite impossible to match.

Below: In some countries before letters can be sorted by an automatic machine, the postcodes must be translated into a series of phosphorescent dots which the machine can read. This picture shows the dots being typed on the letters.

Below: The thin and thick lines of a bar code hold all sorts of information. They are read by a laser pen.

5 000208 001804

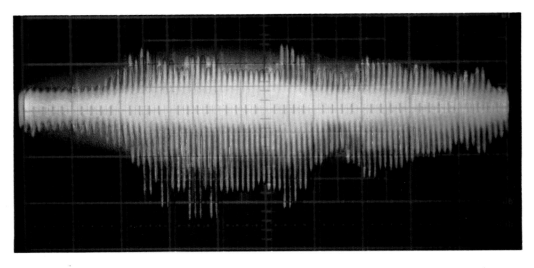

Even people who sound alike have differences in their voices that can be detected electronically. The sounds their voices make can be printed on graphs like this. As with fingerprints, each person makes a different pattern. This voiceprint is of a person saying "Where are you?" It took one second to record.

Teaching Machines to Talk

In science fiction stories, machines have been talking to human beings for many, many years. But what is the real situation? Are talking machines ever likely to be built?

There are two separate parts to this problem. First, the machine must be able to recognize and understand what we are saying. Secondly, it must reply in speech that we can understand. Making a machine talk is easier than teaching it to understand what we are saying.

Simple Talking Machines

There are several kinds of simple electronic talking machines on the market. Calculators can be made to speak the answer to your calculations; speaking machines teach children how to spell. These machines are computers with a small vocabulary of spoken syllables programmed into them. To make a word, the computer takes the necessary syllables from its store and joins them together in the right order – "cal-cu-late."

How We Understand Speech

Have you ever thought how complicated speech is? If we ask a man, a woman and a child to say the word "talk," we will recognize the word without difficulty in each case. But to the computer the differences in the sound of the three versions make it unrecognizable. And we can make things more complicated still by asking a Canadian, a French woman and a Japanese boy to say the English word "talk." We may have to work a little harder at it, but we still recognize the word. The poor computer has no chance at all.

Speaking robots can be fun. This machine asks questions and the child dials in the answers.

Why do we have this amazing ability to recognize different sounds as meaning the same thing? When we learn to talk as babies we begin to recognize different sounds as meaning the same thing. But scientists are still not sure exactly how this happens.

The Computer Compares Sounds

Computers are different. Each speech sound we make can be put down on paper or on a screen as a *voiceprint*. We speak into a microphone and an electronic machine sorts out the sound waves from our voice and makes a kind of graph of them. These sound pictures can be stored in a computer's memory. The computer can then compare the voiceprint of any word it hears with the ones stored in its memory. Unfortunately, as we have seen, no two people speak exactly alike, so the computer has to do a lot of guessing. Scientists have helped by getting a lot of people to say the same words and then asking the machine to make an "average" voice picture of them.

Computers that have been programmed in this way can understand some simple commands. But there is a big gap between a machine understanding a few single words and it understanding proper sentences. How, for example, is a computer

An astronaut talks to the computer that runs the spaceship in the film *2001: A Space Odyssey.*

going to cope with the spoken words "bare" and "bear" or "mail" and "male"? The words sound the same, but we humans know which word is meant because of the words around it.

Scientists have been working on these problems for many years, but they have not yet succeeded in making a robot that can really talk to us. Perhaps we will have to program a computer with all the information in the world about it, just as a baby learns. Then we might have a robot with all the information it needs to make it talk.

The favorite word of the dreaded Daleks in the "Dr. Who" series seemed to be "exterminate."

Computers and Health

The computer has helped to bring about some of the most important advances in medicine in recent years. And, as computers become better and cheaper, they will certainly play a big part in keeping us healthy in years to come.

Computers are used in almost every branch of medicine. They are used by surgeons, physicians, nurses, chemists and people who do the behind-the-scenes office work.

One of the most important uses of the computer is in helping disabled people. A device designed for the blind, for example, is a computerized reading machine. It can scan the words in a book and turn them into electrical pulses which drive a speech machine that "speaks" the words. If the computer arrives at a word which is not in its memory, it simply spells out the letters.

Machines for the Deaf and Dumb

Computers have been designed to help people who are deaf and dumb. One of these is a special board covered with common words, phrases and letters. By touching different parts of the board, the words or phrases appear on a VDU screen, and the machine can be made to say the words. Some of these machines are still rather crude, but advances are being made all the time.

Computers and the Physically Handicapped

To help people who are handicapped in one way or another, computers can be programmed to work machines such as household appliances. Sometimes the patient has very little movement and devices have to be designed that can be worked by small movements of the head or perhaps a finger or toe. Sometimes a tube in the mouth that can be sucked or blown works the computer. When scientists have invented a machine that will really respond to human voice commands, there will be a whole new world of computer-controlled machines for the handicapped.

Finding Out What is Wrong With the Patient

One of the most interesting uses of computers in medicine is programming them to interview patients and find out what is wrong with them. The

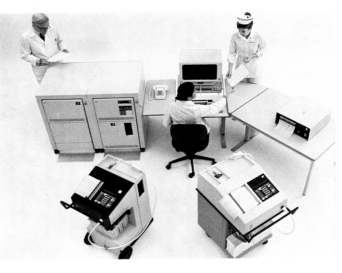

Above: A few of the computerized machines used in a modern hospital.
Below: A doctor explains to medical students the use of an electronic machine that records the patient's heartbeat.

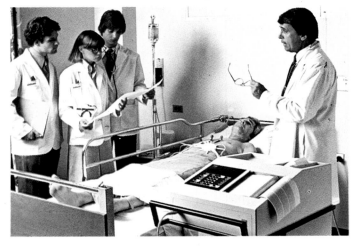

Below: A machine that separates out blood cells. This allows very accurate diagnosis.

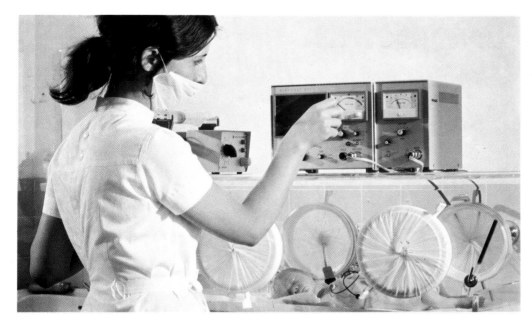

Left: A premature baby is cared for in a warm, germ-free container. Tiny electronic devices fixed to the child continually check heartbeat and breathing and warn of any changes.

computer asks the patient a question, and the patient punches in his or her reply. This goes on until the computer has diagnosed the patient's complaint.

The patient still sees the doctor, but the doctor is helped by the information in the computer, thus saving much of his time. Some studies also show that in certain cases people are more honest in their answers to the computer than to the doctor!

Computers are also proving useful in training medical students in subjects such as anesthetics. Dummies controlled by computers act exactly as a patient would during an operation. Certain things can be made to go wrong with the dummy, and the student has to take the right action – otherwise the computer announces that the patient is dead!

Watching Over Patients in Hospitals

Computers are being used more and more to monitor patients in hospitals. Very sick patients or patients recovering from surgery often need watching over for long periods of time. Their temperature, pulse rate and heart waveforms all have to be monitored constantly. The computer can carry out this job very successfully. As soon as something goes wrong with any of the readings, the computer gives a warning to nursing staff. And one computer can keep watch on several patients at the same time.

As computers become more and more powerful and their programs more wide-ranging, there will certainly be more useful jobs they can do in helping doctors keep us healthy.

Above: A system that aids people with serious speech problems. As different parts of the board are pressed, words appear on the screen.

Below: A foot-operated system helps people who are severely handicapped to use the computer.

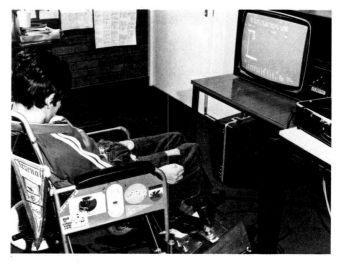

Electronic Telephones

Tomorrow's telephones will be all electronic. If you cannot get through to the person you want to speak to, a robot voice will explain why or tell you what you have done wrong. Telephone systems will be digital and the cables will be fine glass fibers.

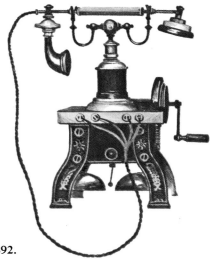

A telephone of 1892.

The world's telephone systems are being overloaded as more and more people want to use them. Vast networks of exchanges, wires and mechanical switches can no longer cope with the ever-increasing telephone traffic. This is why exchanges in several parts of the world are being fitted with electronic instead of mechanical switching. These new exchanges are entirely controlled by computers.

How the Telephone Works

In the old system, when we speak into the telephone, a microphone turns our voice into small varying electric waves. These varying waves go along wires through your telephone exchange, where mechanical switches have routed your call to the right number, to the receiver at the other end. There the electrical waves are turned back into sound waves by a small loudspeaker in the earpiece.

The new telephones use *pulse code modulation*. This is a way of turning analogue (continuously varying) signals like the varying electric waves from your voice, into digital signals – on or off as in a computer's binary system. The electrical waves from your voice are sampled 8000 times a second and a digital value is given to each sample.

Below left: The new telephone has a microprocessor inside it. It can remember 10 numbers and will re-call the last number rung. It also tells the time.
Below: An engineer examining one of the circuit boards in an electronic exchange.

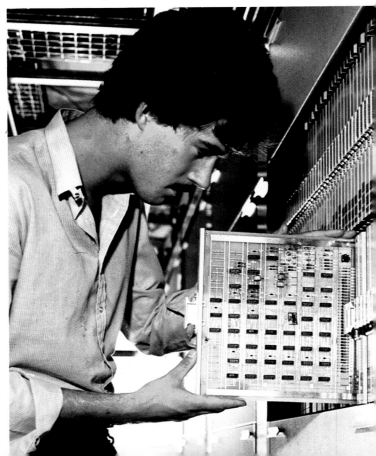

The digital information is then sent along the telephone wires and turned back into continuously varying analogue signals at the other end. The turning into digital signals can be done at the exchange or even in the telephone receivers.

This digital system has many advantages. Noise and distortion are almost completely cut out. Several telephone conversations can be sent along the same piece of wire at the same time. The telephone call capacity of an existing cable can be increased by between 24 and 30 times. And, since computers "talk" to each other in digital language, different kinds of traffic can be sent along the telephone wires at the same time.

Digital Exchanges

Digital telephone exchanges are smaller, faster and cheaper than the old kind. The equipment takes up only a fifth of the space and is much more reliable. Also, fewer people are needed to run them.

Digital exchanges will be able to remember numbers that are used a lot. They will also repeatedly dial a number that is busy and will ring you when it is free.

Behind all this is, of course, the magical silicon chip.

Above: All-electronic telephone exchanges are smaller, faster in operation and cheaper to run than the old mechanical kind.

Below: A computer being used to design the complicated circuits needed in an electronic exchange.

Electronics at War

Today's armies, navies and air forces could not function without the computer and the laser. In both attack and defense they are now vital instruments in all kinds of ways.

The distances which guns can fire are increasing all the time. This means that the problem of finding and hitting the gun's targets is becoming more difficult. Artillery is usually aimed by an observer at the front line who sends his instructions back to the distant gunners. Nowadays, the observer has a small computer keyboard which is linked by radio

Right: A small hand-held computer is being used to calculate accurate firing data for mortars.
Right below: Gun control computer system in a military vehicle.
Below: In modern warfare, speed and accuracy are vital. Here a soldier operates a computer-controlled fire-control system into which can be fed all kinds of data, from wind speed and direction to the exact position of the target.

to a main computer at the gun battery. The main computer may be many miles away. The observer punches into the keyboard certain numbers which describe the exact positon of the target in relation to the observer.

When the computer receives this information it gets to work. Having been given the position, it

allows for wind speed and direction, air temperature and humidity. It even allows for the rotation of the earth and other things which might affect the flight of the shell. This information goes to the gun sights and the gun is fired. The shell lands on the target.

Tracking Enemy Shells

Radar is used to track incoming enemy shells. The radar beam picks up the incoming shell at several points on its flight and a computer calculates its exact flight path. This allows the computer to work out the spot from which the shell was fired. The information is used by the computer to range guns onto the enemy artillery. All this can happen so quickly that counter artillery shells can be on their way before the first enemy shell has landed.

The New Fighting Aircraft

The latest fighting planes are full of new electronics. In the European Tornado aircraft, the second crew member has radar displays with which he can deliver weapons, navigate and maneuver in air combat. Beneath the plane is a laser that sends out a beam to measure the exact distance to ground targets. The crew have other radar systems which can take the aircraft at speed close to the ground, automatically avoiding hills, high buildings, masts and even trees. This allows it to make detection and shooting down by the enemy extremely difficult.

Above: A Sea Dart air defense missile being fired. It is equipped with a radar seeker that homes in on its target.

Laser Ranging

The observer at the front line is only one way of directing gunfire. Once enemy tanks are spotted, a Remote Piloted Vehicle can take off. This is a pilotless aircraft that carries various electronic devices including a television camera. With this camera, the plane fixes on an enemy tank and this works a laser beam that also fixes on the target.

At the same time, guns open up in the general direction of the target, firing special guided shells. These shells carry laser detectors, which once they are in the area of the target, pick up the laser signal reflected from the enemy tank. This laser signal operates a control mechanism in the shells and they home in on the target.

The Tornado is a low-level strike aircraft equipped with all the latest electronic aids to allow it to fly at tree-top height.

Above: Missiles being launched and guided by an unmanned automatic tracker radar system (in the dome). In all weathers and at night the radar can find and follow targets and guide the missiles to them.

Left: An operator marks the tank by flashing a spot of laser light on it. A laser-guided missile detects the spot of laser light on the tank and homes in on it.

Eyes in the Sky

More and more satellites are being rocketed into orbit around our Earth. One of their most important uses is in helping to forecast the weather.

For people such as farmers, fishermen, pilots and builders the weather is vitally important – not only today's and tomorrow's weather, but the likely weather next week or next month.

All over the world, people are constantly recording the weather on land, sea and in the air. These observations are sent around the world to be used by forecasters in a very complicated kind of analysis. Today, most analysis is done by big computers.

Weather Satellites

In recent years, satellites have become one of the most important tools the weather forecaster uses. There are two main kinds of weather satellite. The first is the *geostationary satellite*. This is positioned 22,250 miles (35,800 km) above the Earth's surface, right over the equator. These satellites take 24 hours to go once around the Earth, the same length of time that the Earth takes to revolve once. This means that the satellites appear to stay fixed over one point on the Earth's surface. The pictures they take are always of the same place.

A few geostationary satellites positioned around the equator can cover most of the world

By looking at pictures of cloud formations taken from weather satellites, forecasters can tell a great deal about weather movements. This picture shows a cold front system over Florida.

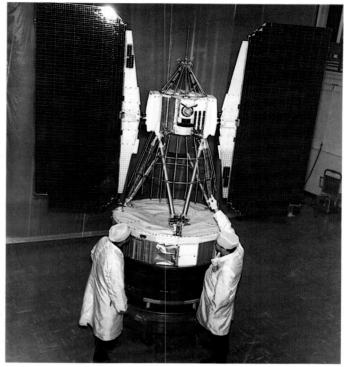

The picture on the left shows an early weather satellite. The one above is bigger and more complicated.

from their great height. They radio pictures down to Earth, and weather forecasters analyze cloud formations and speeds to find out about the warm and cold fronts we hear about in the weather forecasts.

Satellites Over the Poles

The second kind of satellite is the *polar-orbiting* kind. These travel close to the North and South poles at a height of about 500 miles (800 km). As these satellites are moving in a direction different from the Earth's spin, they cover a different part of the Earth every time they go around. Each satellite covers most of the globe every 12 hours. Because they travel quite close to Earth, these satellites are very useful to weather forecasters.

Infra-red Pictures

Satellites take two different kinds of picture. An ordinary picture, similar to that taken by an ordinary camera, shows the position of clouds in the daytime.

The other kind of picture is the infra-red. We know that infra-red rays are rays immediately below the visible light part of the spectrum – infra-red means "below the red." We cannot see infra-red rays but we can feel them as heat. It is infra-red rays produced by an electric toaster that turn our bread brown.

Photographs taken with infra-red rays can be taken in darkness as well as in daylight. They measure the temperature of whatever the camera is aimed at. The whiter a cloud appears in an infra-red picture, the colder it is. Since the temperature tends to drop the higher you go, the colder a cloud is, the higher it is. So the height of clouds can be worked out by using infra-red photography from satellites.

Using the Computer

The computers used for weather forecasting are very big machines. They have to be because of the enormous mass of information that they have to deal with and the number of calculations they have to carry out. Hundreds of weather stations supply information on temperature, wind speed and direction, air pressure and humidity. With all this, the computer calculates what is happening in each square mile of the Earth's surface and what is likely to happen at various times in the future, from one hour to several days or a month from now. Forecasts that cover a week ahead are less accurate than those that cover one- or two-day periods.

But weather forecasting, as we all know, is still far from being an exact science. The weather forecaster still has to study the computer's results and interpret them for us.

To and From Satellites

The space around our Earth is being filled with more and more artificial satellites. These are being used for all kinds of tasks, but most important is their role in communications. With the help of satellites we can now send television pictures and telephone signals all around the world.

Television signals and some radio signals are blocked by the curve of the Earth. But signals sent up to a satellite in space and bounced back to Earth can travel freely from continent to continent. They travel through the atmosphere quite freely.

Radio signals can travel right around the Earth because they bounce back from an invisible band called the ionosphere. The ionosphere is in the upper atmosphere and is made up of electrically charged particles. It is these particles that reflect the radio signals.

Why Satellites?

Television broadcasts have to be sent out on the UHF (ultra high frequency) and VHF (very high frequency) wave bands. These are very short

Above: Telstar, the first communications satellite, launched into space in 1962. It circled the Earth in 90 minutes. Around the middle of the satellite are the microwave antennas which receive and re-transmit the signals from Earth.

Below: Communications satellites are carried into orbit by three-stage rockets. The satellites appear to remain fixed in the sky, always over the same spot on the Equator. The antennas focus the relayed signal into a narrow beam which wastes as little power as possible.

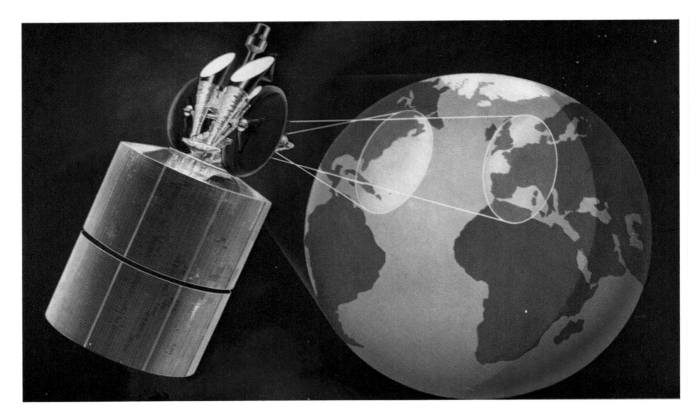

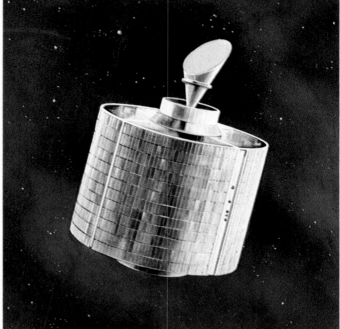

waves, and because they are so short they go right through the ionosphere and are not reflected back to Earth. This is why it is usually impossible to send TV pictures farther than the horizon.

So we need satellites in space to bounce back the television signals to Earth. These signals can be directed back to an area perhaps thousands of miles from the transmitting station.

The Intelsat communications satellites have changed over the years. On this page are shown Intelsat II (above left), Intelsat III (above) and Intelsat IV (below). The electrical power for these satellites comes from solar cells covering the outside of their cylindrical bodies. Only a few hundred watts are generated by these cells but this is enough to power all the electronic equipment. Batteries give reserve power when the satellite is in the Earth's shadow. Notice that the antenna arrangements are different in each.

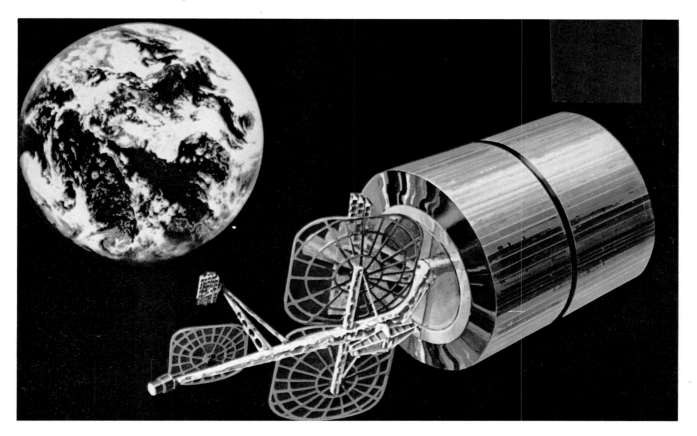

Left: A SATCOM III-R satellite is made ready for launch at the Kennedy Space Center. This satellite gives television, voice channels and high speed data transmission to all 50 states.

Below left: EXOSAT is a scientific satellite. It carries out experiments in X-ray astronomy.

Below: METEOSAT gives information to the weather forecasters on cloud cover, temperature and water vapor.

High in the Sky

The first communications satellite was called Telstar. In 1962 it was fired into an orbit where it circled Earth in about 90 minutes. Because the satellite was in such a low orbit over the Earth, the early television transmissions between Europe and the U.S. lasted only a few minutes before Telstar vanished over the horizon. This made further transmission impossible.

The new communications satellites are fired into geostationary orbit and appear to remain fixed high in the sky, always over the same spot on the Equator.

How the Satellite Works

The American Intelsat communications network is the world's main satellite system. Any country can hire time on this network.

The satellites have been improved over the years, but they all have some things in common. Their antennas are "dish" reflectors. These collect the incoming signals and send out the outgoing signals in a narrow beam.

The main part of the satellite goes round and round, making one complete revolution every second. But the antennas do not rotate with it. They stay fixed in relation to the Earth stations.

There are two reasons for the rotation of the satellite. The first is that anything in space that always faces one side to the Sun gets extremely hot on that side, while its other side becomes extremely cold. Such extremes of temperature can be harmful to the very complicated electronics inside the satellite. The second reason is that the spinning motion stabilizes the satellite and keeps it in position in space.

There are, however, some communications satellites that do not revolve. Their heating problem is solved by giving them a special outer shell. Inside are gyroscope systems to keep them in position. These satellites have wide solar panels like wings which are always kept pointing at the Sun. Electricity manufactured by these panels keeps the satellite's electronic equipment working.

Handling the Signals

Signals are beamed up to the satellite from special ground stations. The satellite gathers the radio waves in its "dish" antennas and amplifies them thousands of millions of times. Then it sends them out again on a different wavelength. Different wavelengths are used for incoming and outgoing signals so that there is no danger of them becoming mixed up.

The signals are received and sent out on microwaves – very short waves (see page 33).

On the Ground

Ground stations have large dish antennas, usually about 98 feet (30 meters) across. These big dishes can be moved to point at any satellite in their part of the sky. The same antenna can be used for both sending and receiving signals because the outgoing and incoming signals are on different wavelengths.

Right above: The LAGEOS satellite is geostationary over the San Andreas earth fault in California. Laser beams from ground stations are reflected back from it and allow scientists to pinpoint any earth movement that might occur.

Right: A big dish antenna used for sending and receiving communications satellite signals. The dome in the background is a radar early warning system for tracking missiles.

Signals from the Stars

Astronomers are reaching further and further out into space as bigger and bigger radio telescopes pick up signals from the remotest parts of the universe.

Stars give out all kinds of energy. They send out not only light waves that we can see, but waves of many different lengths – X-rays, ultra-violet rays, infra-red rays and long and short radio waves. However, the Earth's atmosphere will only let some radio waves through. This means that only radio waves can be studied from the ground. To observe the heavens at other wavelengths, astronomers have to send instruments above the atmosphere in satellites.

Below: This huge radio telescope is at Arecibo in Puerto Rico. Its great dish is 1000 feet (305m) across and is built over a natural hollow in the ground. The antenna is suspended 500 feet (150m) above the dish and can be reached by a catwalk.

Radio astronomers study radio waves coming from space just as "optical" astronomers study the light from space through their telescopes.

Radio Telescopes

The science of radio astronomy began in 1931 when an American engineer, Karl Jansky, was investigating how the atmosphere affected radio reception. He noticed that, as well as hiss from thunderstorms, there was radio "noise" coming from various sources in the sky. Since then, radio astronomy has never looked back. Radio telescopes have grown bigger and bigger, the receivers used have become more and more sensitive, and now there are computers to sort out the results at a rate no human scientist could match.

A radio telescope works very much like any ordinary radio set. But the power of radio signals from space is very very small. This means that special efforts have to be made to collect these faint signals. Special "big dishes" are often used. These

QUASARS

Quasars are bodies that look like ordinary stars when viewed through an optical telescope. But these are no ordinary stars. They send out an enormous amount of energy as radio waves. They appear to send out hundreds of times more energy than ordinary galaxies of stars. The farthest quasars are the remotest objects yet found in space. Some of them are as much as 15,000 million light years away.

PULSARS

Pulsars are strange bodies that give out energy, both as light and as radio waves, in rapid pulses. A pulsar is a rapidly-spinning neutron star. Neutron stars are made up of neutrons, tiny particles that are found in the nuclei of atoms. These stars are so dense that a pinhead of material from a neutron star contains a million tons of matter.

concentrate the radio waves by reflecting them onto the antenna in the center of the dish.

Some radio sources in space send out signals on just one wavelength. Most radio sources, however, send out all wavelengths of waves, so it is not very important where the radio astronomer tunes in.

Different types of antenna systems are used to listen to the stars. In addition to the big dishes that can be steered to face in any direction, there are some that are fixed. Other systems have several small radio dishes in a long straight line. The astronomers let the Earth's rotation swing them into the position they want.

Another approach is to record signals from radio telescopes on opposite sides of the Earth. Both dishes look at the same radio source at the same time. By comparing the results, the astronomers can achieve very accurate detail. It is as though they are using a radio telescope as wide as the Earth.

Right: Astronomers use massive radio telescopes like this big dish at Parkes Observatory in Australia to pick up signals from distant stars. From its infancy in the 1930s, radio astronomy has become one of the most exciting branches of astronomy. It shows astronomers a different kind of universe, inhabited by strange bodies such as quasars and pulsars as well as ordinary stars. This radio telescope, unlike the one on the opposite page, can be pointed to any part of the heavens.

Light that Cuts Steel

A high-powered ruby laser punching a hole in stainless steel. The temperature of the light beam as it hits the steel is about 4800°F (2650°C), hot enough to vaporize the steel and burn a hole only 2/100 inch (0.5mm) across.

The laser is one of the most exciting inventions of the 20th century. It has become the super-tool of science, communications, medicine and weapons systems.

A laser is a device that sends out a narrow, powerful beam of light. This light beam is very special and can be used to perform a wide range of tasks. It can cut through metals at high speed and carry out delicate machining and drilling work on hard and brittle materials. It can, for example, drill a tiny hole in a diamond. It can be used by surgeons to perform delicate operations. It can be used by chemists, surveyors, engineers, and the list of its uses is increasing all the time.

The First Laser

The first laser was built in 1960 by Theodore Maiman, an American scientist. It was quite a simple piece of apparatus – a ruby rod (a fluorescent ruby crystal), around which was coiled a light tube. When the ruby rod was subjected to intense flashes of white light from the tube, it produced flashes of red laser light. But these were no ordinary flashes of red light. They were much more powerful than the white light that caused them.

What Makes Laser Light?

As we saw on page 10, everything is made of tiny atoms. Each atom has a central nucleus, with electrons whizzing around the nucleus at tremendous speed. When we aim light or heat at the

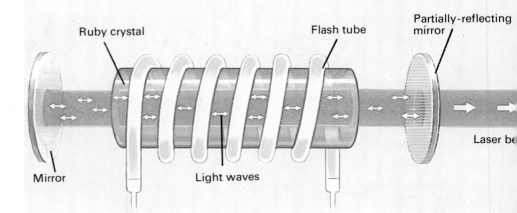

A ruby laser consists of a flash tube wound around a ruby rod. Tiny pulses of light bounce back and forth along the ruby rod from mirror to mirror until a beam of laser light shoots through the partially-reflecting mirror at one end.

Dr. Theodore Maiman, who made the first laser at the Hughes Aircraft Company in California. He is seen here with his ruby laser.

of laser light builds up and shoots out one end of the laser tube.

How Laser Light is Different

Laser light is different from ordinary light in two important ways. First of all, it is very "pure." Ordinary light that comes from the Sun or from a light bulb is made up of all the colors of the rainbow – red, orange, yellow, green, blue, indigo and violet. All these colors have different wavelengths, as we have seen. In ordinary light, all these waves are jumbled up, often interfering with each other.

Laser light is pure because all the photons it shoots out are of the same wavelength. Instead of interfering with each other, they are all in step. They add to each other. Laser light is called *coherent light* and is much more powerful than ordinary light. It can travel much farther.

The other big difference between ordinary light and laser light is that a laser beam is very narrow and hardly spreads out at all. When you point a torch at something, the beam spreads out as it goes outwards. A laser beam is pencil-thin and can be aimed very accurately at a fixed point. Laser light is not wasted.

electrons, they can be made to jump from their normal paths around the nucleus to other orbits further away. Then the electrons spring back to their normal paths and when they do this they give out a small bundle of energy. These bundles are called *photons*. In lasers, the photons are tiny light waves.

In the ruby laser, the flashing white light from the coiled tube excites the electrons in the ruby atoms. Many electrons jump to higher orbits around the nucleus of their atoms. Then one electron flashes back to a lower orbit and sends out a tiny pulse of light. This starts a cascade of light flashes from other excited atoms. An intense pulse

Laser beams have many uses. Here a laser is being used in the construction industry to check the alignment of a tunnel. Since light travels in straight lines, and lasers produce such narrow beams, they provide a perfect way of aligning things.

Using Lasers

The uses of lasers are increasing rapidly year by year. Doctors are using them more and more because the magic laser beam can be very accurate. It is particularly useful in eye surgery and is being used a lot to remove birth marks and tattoos.

Lasers are used to control chemical reactions; to find out the amount of pollution in the air; to send signals along fine glass fiber tubes; to operate checkout systems in supermarkets; to guide missiles to their targets and to find the exact distances between things, from distances of a few yards to the distance from the Earth to the Moon.

Some of these uses for the laser can be seen on these pages.

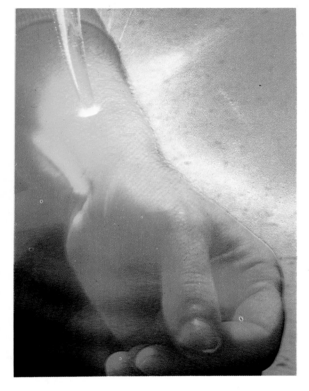

Lasers are being used by doctors to treat some skin diseases (left) and eye complaints (below). Powerful laser beams are used to carry messages to satellites orbiting the Earth (below right). The picture at the bottom takes us into the future. The time may come when a number of powerful lasers mounted on satellites could be used to knock out approaching nuclear missiles.

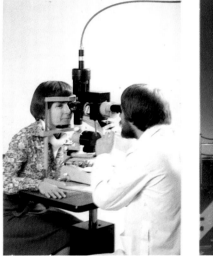

Above: A laser being used to cut canvas. When a laser beam is used to cut fabric, the heat automatically seals the cut edges and prevents them from fraying.

Right: Lasers are used in drilling operations where great accuracy is needed. Here a hole is being drilled in aluminum.

Bottom right and left: In 1969 the Apollo 11 astronauts left a mirror on the Moon. Since then it has been used to make accurate measurements of the distance between the Earth and the Moon. Radar pulses have been bounced off the Moon too, but the radar beams spread out over a vast area.

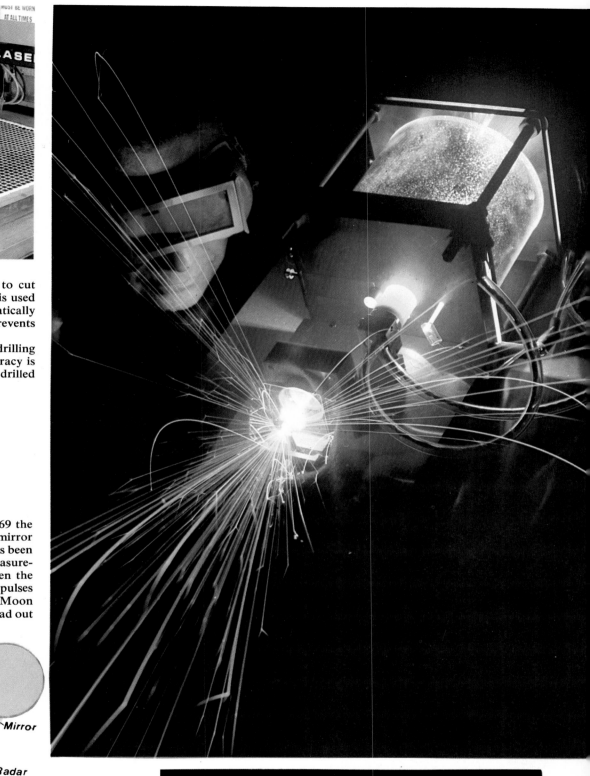

Moon

Mirror

Radar beam

Laser

Earth

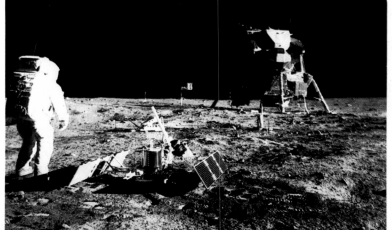

Magic Glass Fibers

A whole new industry has grown up based on "fiber optics." The fibers are hair-thin strands of glass along which pulses of laser light can pass with very little loss. A laser beam sent along a glass fiber can carry much more information than an electric current in a copper cable.

GLASS CABLES

Although laser light is very powerful, it can only be used to communicate between two points if there is nothing in the way. It can be stopped by clouds or fog or other obstacles.

These problems disappear, however, if the laser light is sent along glass fibers. These are hair-thin fibers made of special kinds of glass. Laser light can travel along such fibers with very little loss of power.

Glass has only recently been used to carry messages. The reason for this is that ordinary glass is not very clear. A pane of window glass may look transparent, but when it is seen from the edge it has a greenish-blue color. This coloring is due to the fact that impurities in the glass stop quite a lot of the light from getting through. To make low-loss optical fibers, these impurities must be removed. A piece of the glass used to make optical fibers, nearly a mile thick, would be as transparent as less than an inch of ordinary glass.

Making the Fibers

Not only is it necessary to remove the impurities from the glass to make fibers, it is also necessary to make them from different kinds of pure glass. Each fiber is made up of several layers. The outer layers reflect the light inward more than the layers at the center. This means that as the light travels nearer the surface of the fiber, each layer bends it more nearly parallel to the surface. Hardly any light escapes.

Optical fibers start as glass rods about an inch (2.5 centimeters) in diameter. The rods are heated and drawn out until they are hair-thin fibers miles long.

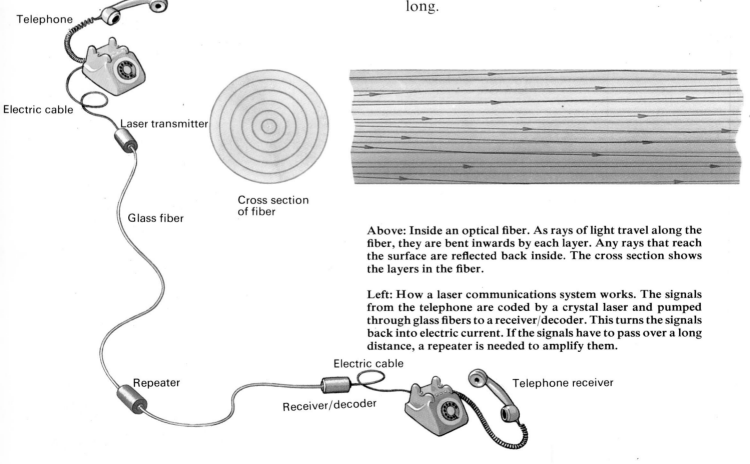

Telephone

Electric cable

Laser transmitter

Glass fiber

Cross section of fiber

Repeater

Receiver/decoder

Electric cable

Telephone receiver

Above: Inside an optical fiber. As rays of light travel along the fiber, they are bent inwards by each layer. Any rays that reach the surface are reflected back inside. The cross section shows the layers in the fiber.

Left: How a laser communications system works. The signals from the telephone are coded by a crystal laser and pumped through glass fibers to a receiver/decoder. This turns the signals back into electric current. If the signals have to pass over a long distance, a repeater is needed to amplify them.

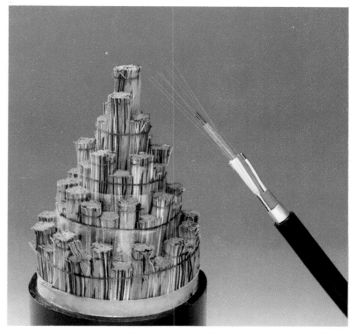

Sending the Light Along the Fibers.

Information sent along fiber optic cables is carried along the fibers by tiny pulses of light. At the input end, the information – telephone conversations, video signals or computer data – is turned into digital (binary) electric pulses which work a laser transmitter. The electrical pulses are turned into light pulses and travel along the fibers to the receiver. The receiver turns the light pulses back into electrical pulses again.

If the signal has a very long way to go, it may have to be amplified on the way. This is done by fitting amplifiers, called repeaters, every 18 to 30 miles (30 to 50 km). (In ordinary copper cables, repeaters are needed about every $1\frac{1}{4}$ miles.)

At present, a single pair of hair-thin glass fibers can easily carry 200 telephone conversations, all going on at the same time. An ordinary copper cable, with 8 pairs of conductors, has a diameter of about 2 inches (5 cm). A glass fiber cable holding 100 fibers is only about half an inch thick, and, of course, very much lighter. The amazing carrying capacity of optical fibers using laser light can be shown by the fact that a single laser could, in theory, be made to allow half the people in the world to talk to the other half, all at the same time!

So, once glass fibers can be mass-produced, they will be used in preference to copper wires. Glass is cheap, plentiful and light. In some cases the reduction in weight will be very important. In modern large aircraft there are many miles of copper wiring that could be replaced by much lighter and cheaper optical fibers.

Above left: A technician joining the ends of glass fibers together. The joined fibers are wound onto drums ready for use in optical cables.

Above right: An optical fiber cable compared with an ordinary electric cable. The electric cable is $3\frac{1}{4}$ inches (8.25cm) in diameter and can carry 6000 telephone conversations. The optical fiber is only a half inch (1.27cm) in diameter and can carry 7680 conversations in just 8 fibers.

Below: The girl is carrying enough glass fiber cable to do the work of the great reel of ordinary copper cable behind her.

Three-dimensional Pictures

Laser light has made possible a new kind of photography in three dimensions. It is called holography. The "picture" is not like an ordinary photograph. It is a transparent piece of film with meaningless light and dark patches on it. But viewed with laser light it becomes almost a "real" object.

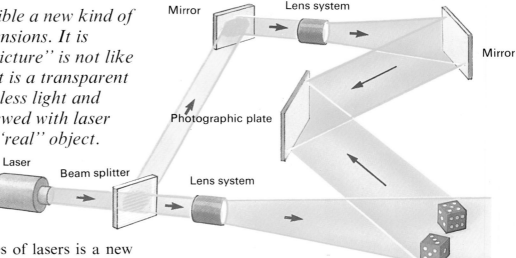

Among the most exciting uses of lasers is a new kind of photography. This is called *holography*. Ordinary photographs are two-dimensional – they have length, breadth, but no thickness. We see them as flat images. But holography can make three-dimensional images, called *holograms*, that look as real as solid objects.

Laser light can be used to make such images because all the light waves in it are the same wavelength and are synchronized or in step.

An ordinary photograph is made by recording the direction from the photographic film of each part of the object being photographed. The amount of light reaching the film from each part of the object is recorded on the film.

In holography, this information is also recorded. But the laser light can also record

Above: To record a hologram, a laser beam is split in two. One beam lights up the object. The other beam follows a separate path to the photographic plate. Here the two beams combine and an interference pattern is recorded on the plate.

Below left: A holographic image. Of course, it is impossible to show what a holograph is really like in a two dimensional picture such as this.

Below: To make a holographic image, the hologram is illuminated with laser light. An observer on the other side of the plate sees exactly the same wave pattern as was used to record the hologram and therefore sees an image of the object. But if the observer moves to one side, the light pattern changes slightly. So the image also changes and it seems to the observer that he is looking at the same three-dimensional image from a different angle. Here two observers are looking at the hologram. They see different views of the object, and the object appears to have depth as well as width and height.

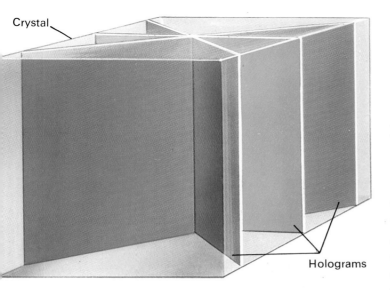

Crystal

Holograms

Above: Holograms can be used to store information. One way of doing this is to record the information on special crystals instead of photographic plates. It is possible to record a number of holograms in a single crystal by recording them on different angles of the planes in the crystal. These angles are represented by the colored sheets in the picture.

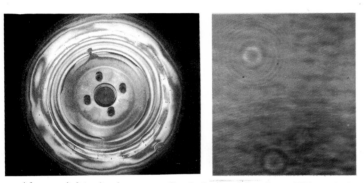

Above right: A close-up of a holographic plate. When it is illuminated with laser light identical to the light used to record the pattern, the observer will see a three-dimensional image.

Above left: Holograms are used to test things. This image of a tire was made by putting a holographic picture of the unpressurized tire on top of an image of the tire under pressure. The differences between the images show the weak spot in the 5 o'clock position.

Below: Holograms can be shown on television screens. A hologram is photographed by a television camera. This hologram is then compared electronically with a previously recorded hologram of the object at rest. The differences between the two holograms show up on the screen. Here, the apparatus is recording the distortion produced in a vibrating guitar.

information about the distance (the third dimension) of each part of the object from the photographic plate. It can record the fact that your ears are farther away than the tip of your nose.

How Holograms Work

Holograms are made by producing two identical laser beams. This can be done either by using two beams or by splitting one laser beam. One beam is directed straight at the photographic plate (usually via several mirrors). This is called the *reference beam*. The other beam lights up the object and this light is reflected from the object onto the photographic plate. When this beam hits the plate it is combined with the reference beam.

But different parts of the solid object being photographed are at different distances from the plate. So, when the light waves from these parts combine with the waves from the reference beam, they are out of step slightly, by varying amounts. (Even light takes time to travel from one point to another.) So the photographic plate records a pattern that contains information about the distance as well as the direction of the amount of light from each part of the object being photographed.

When we look at a holograph plate after a picture has been taken using laser light, we see nothing but a jumble of meaningless dots and circles. But if we shine a beam of laser light through the plate, we see on the far side a three-dimensional image of the object, just as it was when it was photographed. When you look at a holographic image from different angles, it is just as though you are looking at the original object lit by laser light. But if you reach out to touch it, it isn't there.

Perhaps, one day we will have holographic television with apparently real, solid people acting in the corner of our room.

Holography has many other uses. Information can be stored as holograms on film or on special crystals. Holography can also be used to compare the sizes of objects to millionths of a centimeter.

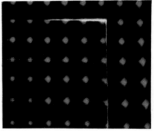

Right: Holograms are useful for storing information. Here several holograms (the red dots) have been recorded on a piece of photographic film.

Seeing With Electrons

Our eyes cannot see things smaller than about 4/1000 inch (0.1 mm). Until three hundred years ago people couldn't see anything smaller than that. Then men started looking at smaller and smaller objects by putting together glass lenses to make microscopes. As time went by, microscopes improved until, by the end of the last century, things as small as 4/100,000 inch (0.001 mm) could be seen through them. These tiny things had to be magnified at least 500 times to bring them to a size that could be seen by the eye.

But this was as far as ordinary microscopes could go. They could not be made to see anything smaller because of the wavelengths of visible light. To see smaller objects, waves with a shorter wavelength had to be used.

The Electron Was the Answer

During the early 1900s it was realized that electrons, the tiny whizzing atomic particles, had a wavelength. And this wavelength was much, much smaller than the wavelength of light. So, the electron microscope was born, using a beam of electrons instead of ordinary light to magnify the objects.

The Transmission Electron Microscope

There are two main kinds of electron microscope: the *transmission electron microscope* (the TEM) and the *scanning electron microscope* (the SEM).

In the TEM, an electron beam is passed right through very thin specimens of whatever is being looked at. The beam is focused by electromagnetic lenses in much the same way that glass lenses focus light. This allows a fine beam of electrons to be focused on the specimen. The electrons go through the specimen and into the microscope's magnetic lenses that produce a much magnified image on a fluorescent screen or a photographic plate.

Transmission electron microscopes magnify things by huge amounts and allow us to see very fine detail. They can enlarge objects so much that we can see things that are only one ten-thousandths of a micrometer across (a micrometer is a millionth of a meter). This is a million times smaller than we can see with our eyes alone. At this magnification, the period at the end of this sentence would be nearly 1600 feet (500 meters) across!

Using the Microscope

Transmission electron microscopes can give detailed information about all kinds of things. Doctors can see how viruses work in giving us diseases such as colds, flu and chickenpox. Viruses are too small to examine with an ordinary microscope.

Tiny things such as viruses can be prepared for examination by mixing them with a coloring stain and looking through them with the electron beam. But bigger specimens have to be cut into very fine

Below: Photographs taken through electron microscopes. The one on the left is a yeast cell budding. Yeast is the substance bakers put in dough to make it rise. A part of the cell swells out and soon becomes a new separate cell. On the right is a bacteria cell. It is called a staphylococcus. These cells cause boils and other kinds of infection. This photograph has a magnification of 175,000.

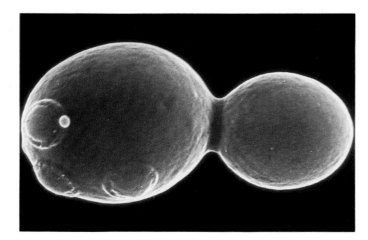

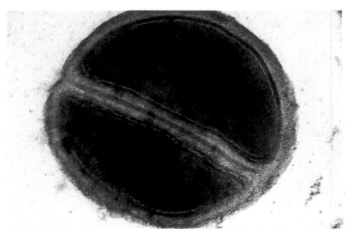

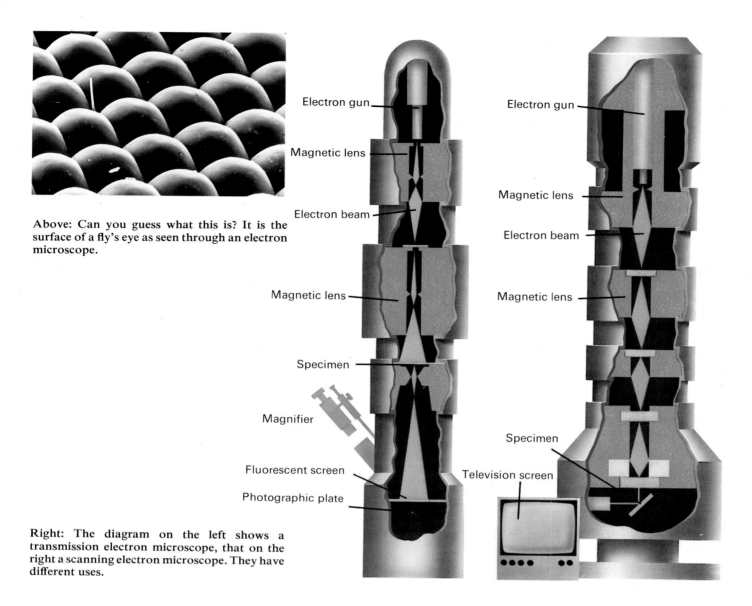

Above: Can you guess what this is? It is the surface of a fly's eye as seen through an electron microscope.

Electron gun

Magnetic lens

Electron beam

Magnetic lens

Specimen

Magnifier

Fluorescent screen

Photographic plate

Electron gun

Magnetic lens

Electron beam

Magnetic lens

Specimen

Television screen

Right: The diagram on the left shows a transmission electron microscope, that on the right a scanning electron microscope. They have different uses.

slices so that the electron beams can go through. These slices are so thin that it would take hundreds of them stuck together to equal the *thickness* of this page.

Most TEMs have electron beams that have voltages of about 50,000 to 100,000. This high voltage is needed to push the electrons through even very thin pieces of material. Some electron microscopes, however, have voltages as high as 1,000,000 to 3,000,000. These are monster instruments more than 20 feet (6 meters) high.

Scanning Electron Microscopes

The other kind of electron microscope, the scanning type, produces a very fine beam of electrons that is swept to and fro across the specimen, just like the beam that zig-zags across a television screen. As the electrons hit the specimen, they throw off other electrons from it. The electrons thrown off depend on the nature of the specimen, and these thrown-off electrons make a picture on a cathode-ray tube.

Scanning electron microscopes are very good for seeing fine details on the surface of objects. They cannot, however, magnify to the same extent as the transmission type. The SEMs have been very useful in the microelectronics industry. They are used to look at the fine details on the surface of silicon chips. The microscope can also be used as an instrument to draw circuits for chips. The electron beam becomes a "writing" tool to produce circuits, guided by a computer.

Some microscopes now combine the most useful features of the scanning microscope and the transmission microscope. If the specimen is thin enough, the electron beam can scan to and fro across it and pick up details inside. This is the *scanning transmission electron microscope* (STEM). It is with this type of instrument that things as tiny as single atoms have been seen.

Inside the Atom

Just as astronomers reach out into depths of space with huge radio telescopes, other scientists are trying to find out more about the inside of the tiny atom. One way of doing this is by sending atomic particles hurling around great machines at speeds approaching the speed of light and making them collide with other particles.

As we saw on page 10, everything is made up of tiny invisible particles called atoms. There are more than a hundred chemical elements, each made up of a different kind of atom.

Only a century ago, the atom was thought to be the smallest bit of matter there was. The word atom means "that which cannot be cut." Then, early in this century, it was found that the atom was made up of a center part or nucleus containing two kinds of particle – protons with a positive electric charge and neutrons with no electric charge. Around the nucleus spins a cloud of electrons, each with a tiny negative electric charge.

But as years went by, scientists kept finding more and more particles in the atom. By bombarding atoms with protons, for example, physicists found they could knock particles from the nucleus and actually change one atom into another.

Big Particle Accelerators

Gradually, more powerful machines called *accelerators* were built to increase the speed of the bombardment. Scientists were staggered to find that all kinds of new particles were given off. In fact, the picture of the atom became so complicated that it could only be "illustrated" with mathematics. At present, over 200 different particles have been found in the tiny atom and no one knows how many more there are waiting to be discovered.

For very high speed beams, machines called *synchrotrons* are used. In these machines, the beam travels in a circle and the particles in the beam are kicked along by powerful electromagnets placed at intervals along the circle. The most powerful synchrotrons are huge. There is one near Geneva in Switzerland that is more than $1\frac{1}{4}$ miles (2 km) across the circle.

Even greater collision force is possible by sending beams of particles in opposite directions around the ring. The beams are kept apart as they gather speed until they are made to collide at a certain point. The particles hit each other with immense force, sometimes producing new particles that can be detected on special machines. Today's accelerators can detect detail down to one ten-thousand-million-millionth of an inch.

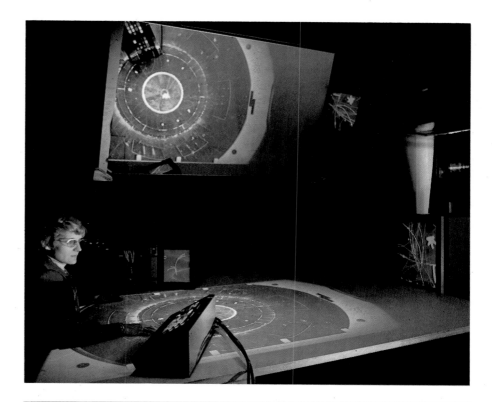

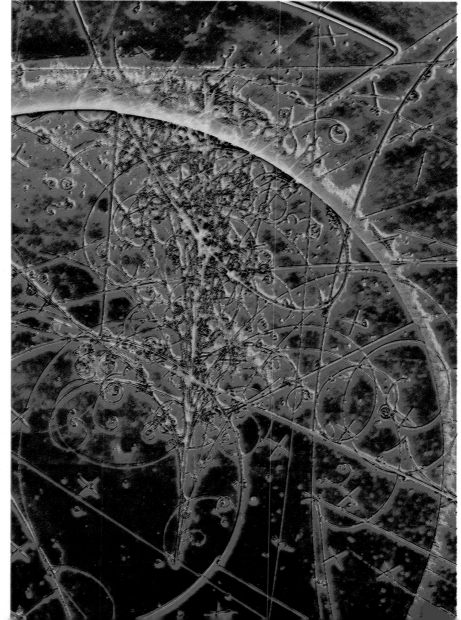

Scientists have found out that the atom is much more complex than was once thought. At one time, it was found to be made up of protons, neutrons and electrons. Now, hundreds of different tiny particles have been discovered inside each atom, and scientists are constantly trying to knock these particles away so that they can find out more about them. To separate particles from the center of the atom, they bombard it with other charged particles from powerful accelerators or atom-smashers.

One of the most powerful of these machines is at CERN, Europe's nuclear research center in Geneva, Switzerland. A small part of this machine is shown in the picture on the left. It is a huge ring over $1\frac{1}{4}$ miles (2km) across. Electric and magnetic fields in the ring are used to speed beams of particles faster and faster around the ring until they are made to hit a target of a chosen substance. The centers of the target atoms break apart into smaller particles and rays. These particles and rays can be seen and measured in special detectors. The picture on the right below shows the tracks of particles in a *bubble chamber*, an instrument that detects the particles. The photograph of the particles is then projected on to a scanning table for examination (top right).

Power from the Atom

The world needs more and more power, and it seems that as time goes by we will get more of this power from the atom.

Some of the electricity we use at home comes from nuclear reactors. These reactors work because heat is given out when atoms of the metal uranium are made to split apart. This splitting process is called *fission*. Fission of the uranium atom happens when it is bombarded by atomic particles called *neutrons*. In the fission process, other neutrons are produced which can go on to split other uranium atoms. So a kind of chain reaction takes place, which makes a lot of heat.

If this chain reaction is not controlled, it can lead to a huge explosion, as in the atomic bomb. But in nuclear reactors, the reaction is kept under control. It is allowed to happen just fast enough to give us useful heat. This heat is used to drive machines that make electricity.

But nuclear fission has its drawbacks. The nuclear fission process, as well as giving out abundant energy, also gives out streams of harmful radiation. Nuclear reactors are surrounded by several yards of concrete to stop this radiation from getting out. And radioactive materials are kept in lead-lined containers. But accidents and leaks have occurred. Many people are worried about the dangers of nuclear fission.

Safe Nuclear Power

The world may still have nuclear power, however, without the dangers of the fission process. It can have this power by using another type of nuclear reaction. This is called nuclear *fusion*. Nuclear fusion is quite different from nuclear fission. It is a process in which different kinds of hydrogen atoms are made to join together, or fuse. When this happens, huge amounts of energy are released. Nuclear fusion is the process that gives the Sun its vast amounts of energy that we experience as light and heat. Inside the Sun and all stars, atoms of hydrogen fuse together to form helium atoms. It is this process that scientists are now trying to imitate on Earth. They have already achieved such fusion, but in an uncontrolled way, in the devastating hydrogen bomb. The problem is to control the fusion and make it give us safe energy.

Trying to Achieve Fusion

Temperatures of millions of degrees are needed before nuclear fusion can take place. Huge machines have been designed to hold the hydrogen by electro-magnets long enough for the reaction to take place. This method has not worked so far.

Other scientists are using powerful laser beams. The laser beams are all aimed from different directions at a tiny pellet of special hydrogen. The powerful beams squeeze the pellet so explosively that it reaches the temperature at which fusion can take place. But so far the scientists have been unable to make the fusion work as they want it to. Hydrogen fuel can be taken from the oceans cheaply and in vast quantities. If scientists can perfect the fusion process, energy will become cheap and plentiful, thanks to beams of laser light.

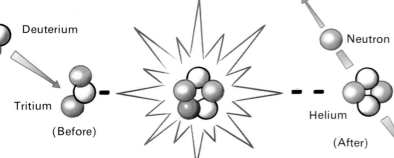

Deuterium

Tritium

(Before)

Neutron

Helium

(After)

Left: In nuclear fusion, deuterium and tritium are forced together. (The two substances are different kinds of hydrogen.) Helium is formed as the atoms explode and neutrons shoot off. All this happens in a millionth of a second.

Laser

Laser amplifier

Right: Fission chain reaction starts when a neutron (black) strikes a nucleus of uranium. The nucleus breaks apart and other nuclei are hit. In a split second, an atomic explosion occurs or the reaction is controlled to make useful power in a nuclear reactor.

Left: The Sun is so hot that the temperature at its surface would turn iron into a vapor in an instant. But even this great temperature is nothing compared to the heat at the Sun's center – about 23,000,000°F (13,000,000°C). When any substance gets hotter, its atoms move faster and faster. The inside of the Sun is so hot that they move very fast indeed and they collide with immense force. This is enough to force atoms together so that their nuclei stick together. It is this fusion (joining together) of atoms that produces the light and heat the Sun and other stars give out. The stream of hot gas thrown out of the Sun at the top of the picture is a dozen or more times as big as the Earth.

Scientists are trying to harness the hydrogen bomb by aiming a number of high-power beams of laser light at a tiny pellet of deuterium and tritium. The high temperature and the great pressure created by the lasers cause a fusion reaction.

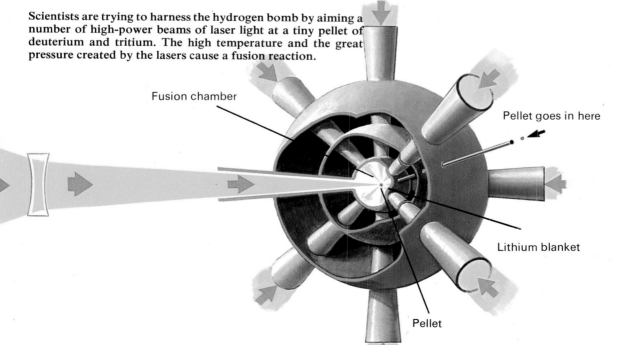

Fusion chamber

Pellet goes in here

Lithium blanket

Pellet

The Home of the Future

Electronics will play a big part in shaping people's lives in the future. Here we look at some of the changes that may occur.

The electronic home of the future may be in a tower as much as 2 miles (3km) high. This may be necessary because of the rapidly increasing world population. The number of people in the world is now about 4500 million. If populations keep on growing as they have in the past, the world could have 10,000 million people by the year 2020.

But there are signs that the population increase slows down as people become richer and better educated. The birth rate in the United States and in most European countries has dropped to a point where almost as many people are dying as are being born.

However, the number of people in the world will go on increasing for many years yet and tower-living may be necessary. Existing material such as reinforced concrete and glass could be used. Travel between tower cities would be by high-speed computer-controlled trains, travelling through interconnecting tubes. The ground areas around the towers could be used for recreation.

Cloud-high tower cities are still a long way off. For some time, most people will live in houses not much different from those of today. But the family home of the future will almost certainly be quite different in some ways. Every household will possess its own computer to cope with the day-to-day running of the home. When properly programmed, it will take over routine tasks such as ordering food as it runs out, paying bills, storing all kinds of personal information such as names and addresses, and keeping details of bank balances and insurance policies. It will also store your favorite recipes and play games with you.

The computer will also act as a master electronic control linked to screens in various rooms. On these screens can be displayed TV programs, electronic newspapers, any information you want from a vast central encyclopedic computer, educational courses, books available in the local library, train times, weather reports and so on.

Mail will also be electronic. You simply type out a letter and send it to an address. There the letter will go into the memory store of your friend's computer, ready for recall at any time, or it can be printed out right away by a high-speed printer.

The family's TV screen will be wall size, made possible by the development of a flat screen. Perhaps they may also have 3D color holography which conjures up a true three-dimensional image of actors or newsreaders in the corner of the room.

Saving Energy

The family house of the future will almost certainly be designed to save as much energy as possible. Insulating materials such as compressed volcanic ash, rigid plastic foams or even paper honeycombs are likely to be used for the inner walls. Solar collector panels can be fitted on the roof. Even in quite cool climates, these can reduce water heating bills by up to 50 percent.

The computer will switch the lights on automatically when the natural light level drops beyond a certain point. To save wasting light in rooms where there are no people, the computer might respond to a movement detector that will tell it whether there are people in the room or not. And, of course, there will be automatic heating, alarm and fire detection systems.

The computer could also control the locks on the door and decide whether to let you into the house or not by comparing your voice with a tape recording in its memory.

The picture above shows what the space colony looks like from a distance. The central hub houses solar power stations and docking facilities for spaceships. There are also mirrors to reflect sunlight to the living areas.

CITIES IN SPACE

Space colonies are now being considered seriously by some people. The one in the picture below is controlled throughout by a big central computer. The colony is positioned 240,000 miles (350,000km) from Earth and about the same distance from the Moon. It consists of a great tube 430 feet (130m) across. This tube forms a ring over a mile in diameter. The tube houses the main living and agricultural areas and can support up to 10,000 people. The big wheel rotates once a minute. This makes an artificial gravity on the surface of the tube away from the center. "Up" is towards the hub and "down" is away from it.

Sunlight is reflected from huge mirrors that can be adjusted to give as much or as little sunlight as required in different parts of the tube. The sunlight also gives the energy to drive the generators which produce the colony's electricity.

Long "spokes" attach the tube to a central hub. At the hub there are docking ports for spaceships and vast antenna arrays for all the colony's communications with Earth.

Is There Anyone Out There?

If we are ever to find out whether there are people on other planets out in space, we or they will probably have to use electronics. The closest star that could have a planet is over 4 light-years away. (A round trip to it would take over 8 years, even if we could travel at the speed of light.) At present, rockets can travel from the Earth at speeds of only about 30,000 miles per hour (50,000 kmph) – about 1/22,500 the speed of light. So a round trip to the nearest star would take 200,000 years!

This shows how difficult it will be for people ever to get to another planet with intelligent beings, or for these beings to come to us. If we ever make contact with other beings, it will probably be by radio signals.

Is other Life Possible?

We know a great deal about how life could have started on our planet Earth. Since 1953, scientists have been able to produce simple proteins, the building blocks of all living things, in their laboratories. In these experiments they imitate the conditions of the Earth's early atmosphere.

Over hundreds of millions of years these simple proteins became more complex and developed into creatures like today's tiny bacteria. These bacteria eventually gave rise to the first simple plants. And so life grew and became more complicated over millions of years until people appeared on Earth.

Life on Other Planets?

If life on Earth came about as a result of such a process, it seems quite likely that life can exist elsewhere in the universe. The more scientists learn about the universe by looking through their powerful telescopes and by using satellites and probes, the more they think there is other life out there somewhere. Radio telescopes have found a host of molecules that could have material capable of making life.

There are almost certainly many planets similar to our Earth among the million upon million planets spread throughout the universe. Could these planets have beings similar to people? We do not know.

Above: Some astronomers have been searching the heavens for signs of extra-terrestrial beings. This coded message sent from the giant Arecibo radio telescope contains all kinds of information that could be decoded by beings on another planet.

Left: This could be the site of one of the first planetary bases on the Martian moon, Phobos. After a while, the whole tiny moon might be turned into an enormous spaceport from which ships could travel far into space.

Messages to Space

In the hope that some intelligent creature may be listening somewhere in the universe, astronomers have sent out coded messages into space. They are also listening for radio signals from space.

But sending messages through space is not easy. Whoever is out there will be beaming signals at various likely stars in turn, not spending too long a time transmitting in any direction. Radio astronomers on Earth are also listening for signals from other stars in turn. There is also a very small chance that our radio telescopes will be pointing at a particular star at the same time that an alien astronomer is beaming a message in our direction.

There is also the problem of tuning in to the right wavelength. We have no idea which wavelength an alien being is likely to use. Some astronomers think that 21 centimeters is possible. This is the wavelength that hydrogen gas produces naturally, and hydrogen is the commonest element in space. Other scientists think that 3.5 millimeters, the natural wavelength emitted by water vapor, could be a likely one.

We just don't know. And, of course, it may be possible that an alien civilization millions of years more advanced than ours will have thought of quite different ways of sending messages through space.

We Send Our Messages

In 1974, the great Arecibo radio telescope in Puerto Rico, sent out a message to the stars. The transmitter was aimed at a cluster of stars called

If we are ever to journey very far into space we must find new and better ways of propelling our spacecraft. All kinds of interplanetary vessels will be designed. Below and right are two gigantic ships of the future.

M13 in the constellation Hercules. The message contained information about the solar system and about people on Earth. This message will travel at the speed of light through space for 24,000 years before it reaches its destination. And if there is no one in M13 to hear it, the message will just go on through space until it leaves our galaxy completely.

The Pioneer 10 and 11 spacecraft which looked at Jupiter and Saturn in the 1970s carry a plaque showing the figures of a man and a woman, and a plan showing the Sun's position in our galaxy.

Voyagers 1 and 2 carry disk recordings giving information about our Earth and the people on it. All these spacecraft are traveling well beyond our solar system and it may just be possible that one day some other being will spot one of them and be curious enough to look.

Glossary

AC See alternating current.

Accelerator, particle An apparatus for bombarding atomic nuclei with atomic particles such as protons.

Access time The time taken to retrieve information from a storage device such as a disk or tape and place it in a computer's main memory.

Accumulator A part of the computer's central processing unit in which results accumulate as numbers and are held temporarily. The numbers are added to, subtracted from or compared with each other.

Address A number that identifies the location in a computer's memory at which a particular piece of data and an instruction code are held.

Alpha particle A particle sent out by many radioactive atoms It is made up of two protons and two neutrons. It carries two units of positive charge.

Alternating current Electric current that rapidly decreases from maximum in one direction, through zero, and then increases to maximum in the other direction. The usual household electricity supply is alternating at 60 cycles per second.

Amplifier An electronic device that increases the strength of a signal such as radio waves or audio waves.

Amplitude The maximum value of an alternating current during a cycle. The higher the amplitude the louder a sound wave, or the brighter a light.

Amplitude modulation (AM) Sound signals can be broadcast by using them to modulate (vary) the amplitude (strength) of radio waves. In AM broadcasts, the amplitude of the carrier waves varies to match changes in the electric waves coming from the radio studio. Electrical interference produces this modulation too. This means that this kind of modulation suffers from background hiss and clicks.

Anode The positive electrode to which electrons travel inside a vacuum tube.

ASCII American Standard Code for Information Exchange. The standard code which allows 128 characters – upper (capital) and lower case letters, numbers 0 to 9, and a range of special characters such as punctuation marks – to be expressed in a computer 8-bit byte. For example, A=65 and a=97.

Assembly language A low-level computer language which represents each instruction performed by the central processor as a short code of letters and numbers. (Compare with *high-level language.*) Assembly language takes instructions from the programmer and turns them into a machine code that the machine can understand.

Atom The smallest part of an element that cannot be divided by chemical means. An atom of any substance consists of a nucleus made up of protons and neutrons surrounded by orbiting electrons. The atoms of the various elements differ in the number of protons, neutrons and electrons which make them up.

Atom smasher The name given to machines such as the cyclotron that accelerate atomic particles to a speed at which they can split atoms.

Atomic number The number of protons in the

Left: An alpha particle shoots out from the nucleus of an atom. It consists of two protons and two neutrons. Below: An amplitude-modulated wave.

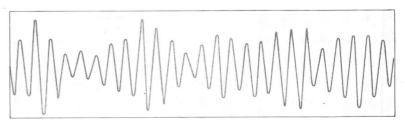

A car battery is made up of several electric cells joined together to give the required voltage.

nucleus of an atom. This is usually the same as the number of electrons orbiting the nucleus.

Audio frequency The frequency of a sound or electrical signal which is in the range of frequencies that the human ear can hear – about 20 to 20,000 cycles per second.

Automaton A mechanical object that can move under its own power. The word is usually used to mean the earlier automatic toys that acted like human beings or animals.

Bar code A pattern of black and white stripes that can be read by a laser scanner. Bar codes are often printed on products such as food packages and cans to identify the products for computer checkout and stocktaking.

BASIC A high-level computer language. It is used more than any other language with microcomputers.

Battery A device that converts chemical energy into electrical energy. Most batteries consist of a series of electric cells. They give out direct current (DC).

Beta-particle A fast-moving electron sent out by a radioactive atom.

Binary A numbering system based on the number 2, as opposed to the normal decimal system which uses 10. Only two symbols, 0 and 1, are needed to express any number. All instructions and data to a computer have to be turned into binary for the computer to understand them. Inside the computer the binary numbers exist as sequences of on-off or high-low pulses of electric current. This is called machine code.

Bit Short for Binary Digit. It is represented by either a 1 or a 0. See byte.

Branch Instruction in a computer program which tells the central processor to leave the normal sequence of instructions and go to another part of the program.

Bubble chamber A chamber used for detecting atomic particles. The chamber is filled with liquid

Right: The numbers 0 to 16 in our decimal system, and their binary equivalents.

Decimal No.	Binary Number
0	0
1	1
2	10
3	11
4	100
5	101
6	110
7	111
8	1000
9	1001
10	1010
11	1011
12	1100
13	1101
14	1110
15	1111
16	10000

Left: A beta particle, which is an electron, is sent out when a neutron in the atom's nucleus changes into a proton and an electron.

125

hydrogen or some similar fluid. The particles heat the fluid along their paths and form bubbles that can be photographed.

Bubble memory A memory chip in which data is stored as tiny regions of magnetism called bubbles.

Buffer A short term computer memory that holds instructions or data until another part of the computer is ready to receive them.

Bug An error in a computer program that may cause the program to work badly or not work at all. "Debugging" means to correct a program.

Byte A group of 8 bits. There are 256 different bytes made by rearranging the 0 and 1 bits.

Camera The front end of a television or video system. It converts an image into a black and white or color picture and then transmits it as an electronic signal which can be seen on a TV screen and/or recorded on magnetic tape.

Capacitor (condenser) A device for storing an electric charge. It is usually formed by two metal plates separated by an insulating layer. It will not allow a direct current to pass, though it will allow an alternating current through, especially if the current alternates very rapidly.

Cathode The negative electrode in a vacuum tube (valve). Electrons flow from the cathode to the anode.

Cathode-rays Electrons flowing from the cathode to the anode in a vacuum tube (valve).

Top: Tracks of atomic particles in a bubble chamber. All the tracks are curved. The faster the particle, the less it curves. Above: A computer is used to analyze bubble chamber photographs.

Right: A variable capacitor. It is used to select or "tune into" a radio station that is broadcasting on a particular frequency.

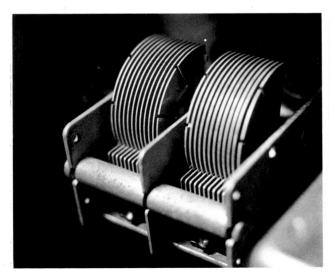

126

Cathode-ray tube (CRT) A video display terminal like a TV set used with computers as an input/output device.

Cell An electrical device used to make electric current by means of chemical change. A simple cell may consist of two different metals immersed in a dilute solution of acid. Cells joined together are called a battery.

Central processing unit (CPU) The part of the computer that joins all the other units together and controls its overall operation. Adding, subtracting and comparing are done in the central processing unit.

Character A term used for any of the letters, numerals, signs and symbols used in computers.

Chip An electronic device in which all the parts such as transistors making up its circuits are contained within one small piece of semi-conductor, usually silicon.

Circuit A complete path through which an electric current flows away from and back to the source of the current, which may be an electric generator or an electric cell.

Clock An electronic device in every computer that produces electric signals at a very fast and regular rate. These signals regulate the running of the computer.

Cloud chamber A chamber containing water vapor, used for detecting radiation. The radiation passing through the vapor produces charged atoms that condense the water vapor and leave a trace that can be photographed.

Coaxial cable Cable for transmitting very high frequency currents. It consists of a copper wire running through and insulated from a copper tube which serves as a second wire.

Cobol A computer language, short for Common Business Oriented Language. It is used a great deal with larger computers.

Coherent light Light in which all the waves are synchronized or in step. Their peaks and troughs coincide and add to each other.

Code number	ASCII character	Code number	ASCII character
32	space	62	>
33	!	63	?
34	"	64	@
35	#	65	A
36	$	66	B
37	%	67	C
38	&	68	D
39	'	69	E
40	(	70	F
41	)	71	G
42	*	72	H
43	+	73	I
44	,	74	J
45	−	75	K
46	.	76	L
47	/	77	M
48	0	78	N
49	1	79	O
50	2	80	P
51	3	81	Q
52	4	82	R
53	5	83	S
54	6	84	T
55	7	85	U
56	8	86	V
57	9	87	W
58	:	88	X
59	;	89	Y
60	<	90	Z
61	=		

Some of the ASCII characters used in computers and their code numbers.

Compiler A program that converts a high-level language such as BASIC into the machine code that actually drives the computer. The compiler translates the whole program into machine code before the program can start.

Conductor, electrical A substance through which an electric current passes easily. Most metals are good conductors.

Cosmic rays Radiation bombarding the Earth's surface from outer space. The rays consist mainly of positively charged protons, with a much smaller number of negatively charged electrons.

CPU Central processing unit of a computer.

CRT Cathode-ray tube.

Data The information that is worked on by a computer. It can be words, numbers or both.

127

Database A large file of data, for instance a set of statistics, that is stored in a computer system. The information is indexed so that it can be used, updated and extended as required in different ways.

Digital A digital system works by producing or using a series of numbers. A digital watch displays the time as numbers for hours, minutes and seconds. Nearly all computers are digital machines because they need data in the form of binary numbers.

Diode A radio valve with two electrodes – a cathode (with heating filament) and an anode. Electrons travel from the hot cathode to the anode only when the cathode is more negative than the anode. A diode therefore allows current to pass in one direction only, so turning alternating current into direct current.

Direct current (DC) A one-way electric current, for example that produced by a battery.

Disk A storage device that allows the computer system to store and retrieve data at high speed. Plastic disks are coated with a magnetic surface on which programs and data are recorded as magnetic patterns.

Electromagnet A bar of soft iron, around which is coiled a wire. Current in the wire turns the bar into a magnet, but the bar loses its magnetism as soon as the current is switched off.

Strong electromagnets are used to lift heavy metal objects such as scrap metal. When the power is switched off, the magnet releases the metal.

Floppy disks are always handled carefully by their covers to prevent dirt sticking to their surface.

Electromagnetic radiation Energy in the form of waves that consist of an electric field at right angles to a magnetic field. Electromagnetic waves include a whole range of different wavelengths that make up the electromagnetic spectrum.

Electron The outermost parts of every atom are made up of negatively charged particles called electrons. A flow of electrons is an electric current.

Electron microscope The ordinary microscope cannot be used to magnify objects that are smaller than the wavelength of light rays. But these tiny objects can be seen by using beams of electrons instead, since electrons act as though they have a wavelength very much shorter than that of light.

Element A substance that cannot be split up into simpler substances by chemical change.

Firmware A computer program that is held in a permanent form, such as on a ROM chip, so that it can be constantly used. Operating systems in most microcomputers are stored in firmware.

Floppy disk A soft disk coated with electronic recording material. These disks are used as additional memory systems in computers.

Flowchart A chart used to develop computer programs. The chart plots information and the order in which it should be used.

Frequency The frequency of any electromagnetic

radiation is the number of waves that pass a given point in one second. A frequency of one hertz (Hz) is equal to one cycle per second. One kilohertz (kHz) is equal to 1000 hertz. The frequency of a sound wave governs its pitch. The frequency of a light wave governs its color.

Frequency modulation (FM) Sound signals can be broadcast by using them to modulate (vary) the frequency (rate) of radio waves. In the radio receiver, the frequency variations of the radio waves are turned back into sounds. The receiver does not detect amplitude modulation caused by electrical interference, so the background noise is very low. This is one reason why FM receivers are used in high quality sound systems.

Gamma-rays Rays given out by some radioactive substances. They belong to the same electro-magnetic family as light waves and X-rays, but they have a much shorter wavelength.

Graphics The production of pictures and diagrams by a computer. The pictures and diagrams are made up of formations of small graphics characters of various shapes and colors.

Grid An electrode in a valve or cathode-ray tube used to control the flow of current through it.

Hardware The machines that make up a computer system, as opposed to the programs needed to operate it. Anything you can actually touch is hardware.

Hertz (Hz) A unit for measuring frequency. See frequency.

High-level language A computer programming language that uses a single instruction to represent a whole group of instructions that the central processor actually carries out. The high-level

Graphics play an important part in today's use of computers. They can be produced by a screen or by a printer.

language may be in English words or groups of symbols.

Holography A method of reproducing 3-D pictures by using a laser beam instead of a camera.

Infra-red rays Radiation given off by warm bodies such as fires or human beings. The rays are not visible to the human eye but can be photographed on special film. The wavelength of infra-red rays is just longer than those of visible light.

Input Programs or data that are fed into a computer. Input units include keyboards.

Instruction A command given in a computer program which produces action by the computer. Instructions are written by the programmer. These are taken by the compiler in the computer and translated into machine code intructions which the machine can understand.

Integrated circuit A silicon chip on which all the necessary components such as transistors, resistors and capacitors have been etched in miniature.

Ion An atom or group of atoms that have an electrical charge. The electric charge is caused by the loss or gain of electrons. An atom with fewer electrons than protons is positively charged; one with more electrons than protons has a negative charge.

A frequency-modulated radio wave. Frequency-modulation (FM) is used in high quality sound systems.

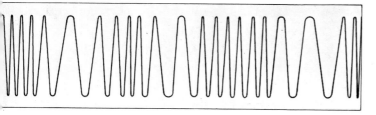

Mainframe computers such as the one above can store and handle vast amounts of information.

K Commonly used measurement of memory size in computers. Though it comes from the metric "kilo" meaning a thousand, 1K is one kilobyte or 1024 bytes.

Laser A device that produces an intense beam of light. The beam is very narrow, coherent (all its waves are in step) and of a single color.

Light A section of the electromagnetic family of waves to which the human eye is sensitive. Visible light covers a range of wavelengths, the longest of which produces the color red and the shortest of which produces the color violet. Light travels at a speed of 186,000 miles (300,000 kilometers) per second in empty space.

Location A part of a computer memory unit containing a particular instruction code or some data. Each location has an address to identify it in order to retrieve its contents.

Loop A set of computer instructions that is repeated until some given condition is satisfied.

Loudspeaker A device that turns electrical currents into sound waves that can be heard.

Machine language The binary coded instructions which the central processing unit of a computer can recognize.

Magnetic tape An inexpensive way of storing data. It is slower than disk storage.

Mainframe A large computer that needs its own air-conditioned room.

Medium wave A radio wave with a wavelength between 200 and 1000 meters.

Mega- A prefix meaning "million." A megabit is a million bits, a megabyte is a million bytes, a megawatt is a million watts.

Meter The main unit of length in the metric system. It was originally intended to equal one ten-millionth of the distance from the North Pole to the Equator. A meter is 39.37 inches.

Microcomputer A small computer containing a microprocessor to which larger peripheral units may be connected. In a home microcomputer, these often include a television set and a cassette player.

Microphone A device which converts sound waves into electrical currents. It is used in telephone transmitters, radio, tape recorders, etc.

Microprocessor A complete central processing unit contained in one silicon chip.

Microwaves Very short radio waves with wavelengths of about 0.1 to 30 centimeters.

Modem A device that enables computers to be connected by telephone wires. It converts the computer's electronic digital signals into analogue signals such as audio signals that can travel along a telephone line. Another modem at the other end of the line will turn the analogue signals back into digital signals for the receiving computer.

Modulation Putting signals (speech or music) on a radio wave. The wave on which they are imposed is called the carrier wave.

Nanosecond One thousand millionth of a second.

Neutron An uncharged atomic particle found in the center of all atoms except hydrogen. It has a fairly large mass – nearly 1840 times as heavy as an electron.

Nucleus, atomic The positively charged center of an atom. It is made up of one or more protons and, except for hydrogen, one or more neutrons. Practically all the weight of an atom is in its nucleus.

Oscilloscope An electronic instrument in which an electric signal or anything that can be reduced to an electric signal is displayed as a "trace" by a spot of light moving on a cathode-ray-tube screen.

Output The processed data or other information that the computer presents through output units. Output units include video screens and printers.

Peripherals Input, memory or output units that may be temporarily connected to the central processing unit. Peripherals include printers and disk drives.

Photoelectric cell A device in which electrons are given out, or in which the electrical resistance changes, when light falls on it. The current passing through such a cell varies according to the brightness of the light. The current can therefore be used to measure the amount of light falling on the cell.

Photon A tiny "packet" of electromagnetic radiation. It can be thought of as a short train of waves of a particular wavelength.

A computer operator loads a magnetic tape into a tape drive unit.

Potential difference Another name for voltage difference. The potential difference between two ends of a conductor results in a flow of electrical current.

Program A complete set of instructions that enable the computer to solve a particular problem or undertake a particular task when given the data required. A computer also contains several permanent programs that operate its various units.

Proton A positively charged atomic particle found in the nuclei of all atoms. The positive charge on a proton is equal to the negative charge on an electron. Protons have a mass slightly less than that of neutrons.

Radar Short for Radio Direction and Ranging, a system in which radio pulses are sent out and reflected back by any objects in their path. The returning pulses are recorded on a screen and their distance found by measuring the time taken for the radio pulses to get to the object and back.

Radioactivity A substance whose atoms break up by themselves, not as the result of an outside force, is said to be radioactive. The radioactive substance usually gives out alpha- and beta-particles, or gamma rays.

RAM Random Access Memory. A computer memory in which programs and data are held temporarily, and in which any instruction or data may be instantly retrieved or changed.

Real-time A computer system that can give the user immediate answers via a terminal.

Rectifier Any device which turns alternating current into direct current by presenting a greater resistance to a current flowing in one direction than to one flowing in the other.

Register A small memory unit within the central processing unit of a computer. It is used for the temporary holding of data, instructions and results.

Resistance The property of an electrical circuit that opposes the flow of current passing through it. Resistance is measured in ohms and is

Above: This robot wears plastic overalls as it sprays bicycle frames. Even robots can be affected by fine paint spray in the atmosphere. Right: This early robot was designed for an exhibition in 1932.

calculated by dividing the voltage (in volts) by the current (in amps).

ROM Read-Only Memory in a computer. A memory that has its program permanently fixed into it and which cannot be changed by the user. The computer can never write any information into this memory.

Semiconductor A substance such as silicon or germanium which is neither a good conductor of electricity nor a good insulator. Transistors are made from semiconductors.

Software The programs that make computers operate. Software is contrasted to the hardware of the actual computer machinery.

Sonar A system of underwater location and direction-finding. Objects are located when they reflect back an "echo" of ultrasonic waves. (Compare with *radar*.)

Spectroscope An instrument for splitting up light into its different colors and studying the spectrum so produced.

Spectrum The series of color bands obtained when light is split up into its rainbow colors. The spectrum of white light is a range of colors and each part of the spectrum is a different wavelength.

Static electricity A stationary electric charge – for example, that produced by rubbing a glass rod with a silk cloth.

Terminal An input/output device linked directly to the computer. The most common terminal is a keyboard and screen.

Time-sharing The sharing of one computer system between several users. Each user has access to the central processor to run their own programs.

Transformer A device for converting alternating current at one voltage to alternating current at another voltage. It consists of a primary coil and a secondary coil, wound separately on a soft iron core. Currents in one coil produce currents in the other coil, and the ratio of the voltages in each is equal to the ratio of the number of turns in each coil.

Transistor A semiconductor electronic device that can amplify or rectify current. Transistors are the main parts in integrated circuits.

Triode An electronic valve with three electrodes inside it – an anode, a cathode and a control grid. It can be used to amplify varying electric currents.

Ultraviolet radiation Light waves which are of smaller wavelength than the light at the violet end of the visible spectrum.

VHF Very high frequency radio waves.

Videotex A system which allows a television owner to communicate with a computer system, and have chosen pages of information sent down a telephone line and projected on the TV screen.

Visual display unit (VDU) A computer output unit consisting of a cathode ray tube video screen.

Voice recognition A system that allows people to give the computer instructions and data by speaking.

Voice synthesis The production of artificial voice sounds which enable the computer to speak.

Volt The unit of voltage (electromotive force and potential difference). It is defined as the potential difference between two points in a conductor if 1 joule of work is done when 1 coulomb of charge passes between them.

Voltaic cell A simple electric cell which produces an electric current by means of two plates of different metals in acid or other chemicals.

Watt Unit of electrical power. It is defined as the rate of work done in joules per second, and is equal to the current in amperes times the voltage.

Wavelength The distance from the crest of one wave to the crest of the next. Radio wavelengths are measured in meters. The wavelength is equal to the speed of the wave divided by its frequency.

Word The central processor of a computer handles bits in groups of a set length called a word. The longer the word, the greater the computer's power. Word lengths can be of 4, 8, 16, or 32 bits. Most microcomputers work in 8-bit or 16-bit words.

Word processor A special computer system designed to handle text and considerably speed up the typing process.

X-rays Electromagnetic waves which have a very short wavelength. X-ray photography is widely used in hospitals for detecting broken bones, ulcers, appendicitis and so on.

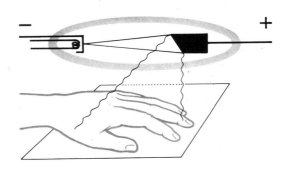

Above: In an X-ray tube, the high positive charge on the anode attracts electrons at high speed. When the electrons hit the anode, X-rays are sent out. These rays leave the tube and can be used to make an X-ray picture on a sheet of photographic film.

Index

ACKNOWLEDGEMENTS

Pages 2/3 middle Science Photo Library, 4/5 IBM, 8 top Met. Office, bottom Rediffusion, 9 top left C.O.I., top right Logica Ltd, middle Computer Aided Design, bottom McDonnel Douglas UK Ltd., 14 Paul Brierley, 15 top Science Photo Library, bottom left & right Paul Brierley, 17 top Mansell, 18 bottom left British Telecom, bottom right Daily Telegraph, 19 (background) NASA, 30 Marconi Electronics, 31 Boeing, 34 Middlesex Hospital, 35 EMI Medical Ltd., 36 bottom Science Museum, London, 37 Science Museum, London, 38 Science Museum, London, 39 left British Telecom, right Ferranti Archives, bottom right IBM, 40 top Atari, bottom NASA, 41 top Photri/Zefa, middle Computer Aided Design, Cambridge, bottom Department of Industry, 42 Hewlett Packard, 43 top BBC Radiovision, bottom Department of Industry, 44 top & bottom BBC Radiovision, 45 Science Museum, London, middle, bottom right & left IBM, 47 top BBC Radiovision, bottom IBM, 48 Apple Computers, 49 BBC Radiovision, 56 Chubb Lock & Safe, 58 Atari, 59 top Zefa, bottom left Sinclair Research, right Tilbury Sandford Brysson Ltd, 60 top McDonnell Douglas, bottom Anadex Ltd., 61 top Ford Motor Co. Ltd., middle Computer Aided Design, bottom & side T.S.B. 62 Boeing., 63 Rediffusion Simulators Ltd, 64 top & bottom Rediffusion Simulators Ltd, 66 Ford Motor Co., 67 Lucasfilm Ltd (LFL) 1983 All rights reserved, 68 top Unimate Ltd, 70 IBM, 71 top left & right Commodore Computers, bottom Cambridgeshire Computer Centre, 72 top Chubb Alarms, bottom Crown copyright, COI, 73 Chubb Alarms, 74 Ceefax, 75 top & bottom British Telecom 76 & 77 Barclays Bank Picture Library, 78 top Hewlett Packard, bottom British Telecom, 79 British Telecom, 80 top left & right IBM, bottom ITT Business Machines, 81 Datasolve Ltd, 82 top & middle National Westminster Bank PLC, bottom Post Office, 83 Post Office, 84 top Paul Brierley, bottom Dr. M. Freeman, 85 top MGM, bottom BBC, 86 IBM, 87 top Seimens Ltd, middle & bottom B.S.C., 88 British Telecom, 89 British Telecom, 90–93 Marconi Space & Defence, 94 NASA, 95 NASA, 96 top NASA, bottom British Telecom, 97 British Telecom, 98 top NASA, bottom left & right Marconi Space & Defence, 99 top NASA, bottom British Telecom, 100 Arecibo Observatory, National Astronomy & Ionosphere Centre, 101 CSIRO, Australia, 102 Hughes Aircraft Co., 103 Hughes Aircraft Co, bottom Mowlem Ltd., 104 top lejt John Hillelson/Howard Sochurek, middle Coherent UK Ltd., right Photri, USA 105 top left Lasercut Products Ltd., right Photri, USA, bottom NASA, 107 British Telecom, 108 Bergstrom & Boyle Ltd, 109 top & bottom left University of Loughbrough, top right Paul Brierley, bottom right Photri, 110 Gene Cox, 111 Gene Cox, 112 CERN, 113 CERN, 115 Lick Solar Observatory, 118 NASA, 126 top & middle CERN, bottom Paul Brierley, 128 top IBM, 129 BBC, 130 ICL Ltd, 131 ICL Ltd., 132 Trallfa Ltd., 133 Hulton Picture Library, 135 Department of Industry.

Picture Research: Penny Warn.